WITHDRAWN

MARSHA NORMAN wrote GETTING OUT (her first play) two years ago in her native city of Louisville, where it premiered in November of 1977 at the Actors Theatre of Louisville. Last year GETTING OUT was produced at the Mark Taper Forum, and was voted the Best New Play (Regional) by the American Critics Association. Her second play, THIRD AND OAK, was presented at ATL last March and subsequently taped by "Earplay" for national airing. CIRCUS VALENTINE, her next work, opened this past season at ATL. Marsha Norman has also written for television and just completed a drama for "Visions" for KCET in Los Angeles. She is playwright-in-residence at ATL under a grant from the National Endowment for the Humanities and has received a Rockefeller Playwright in Residence Award. The idea for GETTING OUT came from her experience working with children in a state mental hospital.

Gramley Library
Salem College
Winston-Salem, NC 27108

WITHDRAWN

GETTING OUT

MARSHA NORMAN

 A BARD BOOK/PUBLISHED BY AVON BOOKS

Gramley Library
Salem College
Winston-Salem, NC 27108

Originally Produced by Actors Theatre of Louisville, Inc. in Louisville, Kentucky

The West Coast Premiere of "Getting Out" was Produced by The Center Theatre Group of Los Angeles Mark Taper Forum, Gordon Davidson, Artistic Director

Originally Produced in New York by the Phoenix Theatre

Produced Off-Broadway in New York City by Lester Osterman, Lucille Lortel and Marc Howard

CAUTION: Professionals and amateurs are hereby warned that "Getting Out," being fully protected under the Copyright Laws of the United States of America and all other countries of the Berne and Universal Copyright Conventions, is subject to royalty. All rights, including but not limited to, professional, amateur, recording, motion picture, recitation, lecturing, public reading, radio and television broadcasting and the rights of translation into foreign languages are strictly reserved, permission for which must be secured in writing from the Author's agent, William Morris Agency, Inc., 1350 Avenue of the Americas, New York, New York 10019, Attention: Samuel Liff and, with respect to amateur stage rights for the United States and Canada, inquiries should be directed to the Dramatists Play Service, Inc., 440 Park Avenue South, New York, New York 10016.

AVON BOOKS
A division of
The Hearst Corporation
959 Eighth Avenue
New York, New York 10019

Copyright © 1978, 1979 by Marsha Norman
Published by arrangement with the author
Library of Congress Catalog Card Number: 79-56243
ISBN: 0-380-75184-4

All rights reserved, which includes the right
to reproduce this book or portions thereof in
any form whatsoever. For information address
Lucille Lortel Productions, Marc Howard,
1650 Broadway, New York, New York 10019

First Bard Printing, February, 1980

BARD IS A TRADEMARK OF THE HEARST CORPORATION
AND IS REGISTERED IN MANY COUNTRIES AROUND THE
WORLD, MARCA REGISTRADA, HECHO EN U.S.A.

Printed in the U.S.A.

GETTING OUT

ARLIE is the violent kid ARLENE was until her last stretch in prison. In a sense, she is ARLENE's memory of herself, called up by her fears, needs and even simple word cues. ARLIE's life should be as vivid as ARLENE's if not as continuous. There should be hints in both physical type and gesture that ARLIE and ARLENE are the same person seen at different times in her life. They both speak with a country twang, but ARLENE is suspicious and guarded, withdrawal is always a possibility. ARLIE is unpredictable and incorrigible. The change seen in ARLIE during the second act represents a movement toward ARLENE, but the transition should never be complete. Only in the final scene do they acknowledge and appreciate each other's presence.

The life in the prison "surround" needs to convince without distracting.

—M.N.

Cast

ARLENE .... late twenties
ARLIE .... ARLENE as a teenager
BENNIE .... former prison guard, looks about fifty
2 GUARDS ....
DOCTOR ....
MOTHER........................ ARLENE's Mother
SCHOOL PRINCIPAL .... woman in her fifties
RONNIE .... teenager
CARL .... punk, in his late twenties
WARDEN ....
RUBY .....ex-con neighbor of ARLENE, in her thirties

Both acts are set in a dingy one-room apartment. There is a twin bed and one chair, but no other furniture. There is a sink, an apartment-size combination stove and refrigerator and a counter with cabinets above. Dirty curtains conceal the bars on the outside of the single window. There is one closet and a door to the bathroom. The door to the apartment opens into a hall. This is a second floor apartment, but the stairs need not be seen.

A catwalk stretches above the apartment and several prison areas connect to it by stairways. There is one cell, stage right, complete with toilet, bed and bars in the first act, and stripped for maximum security in the second. An apron downstage completes the enclosure of the apartment in playing areas for the past.

These announcements will be broadcast beginning five minutes before the houselights come down for Act I. A woman's voice is preferred, a droning loudspeaker tone is essential.

LOUDSPEAKER: Kitchen workers, all kitchen workers report immediately to the kitchen. Kitchen workers to the kitchen. The library will not be open today. Those scheduled for book checkout should remain in morning work assignments. Kitchen workers to the kitchen. No library hours today. Library hours resume tomorrow as usual. All kitchen workers to the kitchen.

Frances Mills, you have a visitor at the front gate. All residents and staff, all residents and staff . . . do not, repeat, do not, walk on the front lawn today or use the picnic tables on the front lawn during your break after lunch or dinner.

Your attention please. The exercise class for Dorm A residents has been cancelled. Mrs. Fischer should be back at work in another month. She thanks you for your cards and wants all her girls to know she had an eight-pound baby girl.

Doris Creech, see Mrs. Adams at the library before lunch. Frances Mills, you have a visitor at the front gate. The Women's Associates' picnic for the beauty school class has been postponed until Friday. As picnic lunches have already been prepared, any beauty school member who so wishes may pick up a picnic lunch and eat it at her assigned lunch table during the regular lunch period.

Frances Mills, you have a visitor at the front gate. Doris Creech to see Mrs. Adams at the library before lunch. I'm sorry, that's Frankie Hill, you have a visitor at the front gate. Repeat, Frankie Hill, not Frances Mills, you have a visitor at the front gate.

GETTING OUT

Act I

[*The* WARDEN's *voice on tape is heard in the blackout.*]

WARDEN'S VOICE: The Alabama State Parole Board hereby grants parole to Holsclaw, Arlene, subject having served eight years at Pine Ridge Correctional Institute for the second-degree murder of a cabdriver in conjunction with a filling station robbery involving attempted kidnapping of attendant. Crime occurred during escape from Lakewood State Prison where subject Holsclaw was serving three years for forgery and prostitution. Extensive juvenile records from the state of Kentucky appended hereto.

[*As* WARDEN *continues, light comes up on* ARLENE, *walking around the cell, as if waiting to be picked up for the ride home.* ARLIE *is visible, but just barely, downstage center.*]

WARDEN'S VOICE: Subject, now considered completely rehabilitated, is returned to Kentucky under interstate parole agreement in consideration of family residence and appropriate support personnel in the area. Subject will remain under the supervision of Kentucky parole officers for a period of five years. Prospects for successful integration into community rated good. Psychological evaluation, institutional history and health records attached in Appendix C, this document.

BENNIE'S VOICE: Arlie!

[ARLENE *leaves the cell, light comes up on* ARLIE,

Gramley Library 11
Salem College
Winston-Salem, NC 27108

*seated downstage center. She tells this story rather
simply. She enjoys it, but its horror is not lost on her.
She may be doing some semi-absorbing activity such
as painting her toenails.*]

ARLIE: So, there was this little kid, see, this creepy little
fucker next door. Had glasses an somethin wrong with
his foot. I don't know, seven, maybe. Anyhow, ever
time his daddy went fishin, he'd bring this kid back
some frogs. They built this little fence around em in
the back yard like they was pets or somethin. An we'd
try to go over an see em but he'd start screamin to his
mother to come out an git rid of us. Real snotty like. So
we got sick of him bein such a goody-goody an one
night me an June snuck over there an put all his dumb
ol frogs in this sack. You never heared such a fuss.
[*Makes croaking sounds.*] Slimy bastards, frogs. We
was plannin to let em go all over the place, but when
they started jumpin an all, we just figured they was
askin for it. So, we taken em out front to the porch an
throwed em one atta time out into the street. [*Laughs.*]
Some of em hit cars goin by but most of em just got
squashed, you know, runned over? It was great, seein
how far we could throw em, over back of our backs an
under our legs an God, it was really fun watchin em fly
through the air then splat [*Claps hands.*] all over somebody's car window or somethin. Then the next day, we
was waitin an this little kid comes out in his back yard
lookin for his stupid frogs an he don't see any an he
gets so crazy, cryin an everything. So me an June goes
over an tells him we seen this big mess out in the street,
an he goes out an sees all them frogs' legs an bodies an
shit all over everwhere, an, man, it was so funny. We
bout killed ourselves laughin. Then his mother come
out and she wouldn't let him go out an pick up all the
pieces, so he jus had to stand there watchin all the cars
go by smushing his babies right into the street. I's
gonna run out an git him a frog's head, but June yellin
at me, "Arlie, git over here fore some car slips on them

frog guts an crashes into you." [*Pause.*] I never had so
much fun in one day in my whole life.

[ARLIE *will remain seated as* ARLENE *enters the apartment.*

*It is late evening. Two sets of footsteps are heard com-
ing up the stairs.* ARLENE *opens the door and walks
into the room. She stands still, surveying the littered
apartment.* BENNIE *is heard dragging a heavy trunk up
the stairs.* BENNIE *is wearing his guard uniform. He is
a heavy man, but obviously used to physical work.*]

BENNIE: [*From outside*] Arlie?

ARLENE: Arlene.

BENNIE: Arlene? [*Bringing the trunk just inside the door*]

ARLENE: Leave it. I'll git it later.

BENNIE: Oh, now, let me bring it in for you. You ain't as
strong as you was.

ARLENE: I ain't as mean as I was. I'm strong as ever. You
go on now. [*Beginning to walk around the room*]

ARLIE: [*Irritated, as though someone is calling her*] Lay
off! [*Gets up and walks past* BENNIE *out the apartment
door.*]

BENNIE: [*Scoots the trunk into the room a little further.*]
Go on where, Arlie?

ARLENE: I don't know where. How'd I know where you'd
be goin?

BENNIE: I can't go til I know you're gonna do all right.

ARLENE: Look, I'm gonna do all right. I done all right
before Pine Ridge, an I done all right at Pine Ridge.
I'm gonna do all right here.

BENNIE: But you don't know nobody. I mean, nobody
nice.

ARLENE: Lay off.

BENNIE: Nobody to take care of you.

ARLENE: [*Picking up old newspapers and other trash
from the floor*] I kin take care of myself. I been doin
it long enough.

BENNIE: Sure you have, an you landed yourself in prison
doin it, Arlie girl.

ARLENE: [*Wheels around, won't this guy ever shut up?*] Arlie girl landed herself in prison. Arlene is out, O.K.?

BENNIE: Hey, now, I know we said we wasn't gonna say nuthin about that, but I been lookin after you for a long time. I been watchin you eat your dinner for eight years now. I got used to it, you know?

ARLENE: Well, you kin jus get unused to it.

BENNIE: Then why'd you ask me to drive you all the way up here?

ARLENE: I didn't, now. That was all your big ideal.

BENNIE: And what were you gonna do? Ride the bus, pick up some soldier, git yourself in another mess of trouble?

ARLIE: [*Struts back into the apartment from the closet door, going over as if to a soldier sitting at a bar.*] O.K., who's gonna buy me a beer?

ARLENE: You oughta go by Fort Knox on your way home.

ARLIE: Fuckin soldiers, don't care where they get theirself drunk. [*Stops.*]

ARLENE: You'd like it.

ARLIE: Well, Arlie girl, take your pick.

ARLENE: They got tanks right out on the grass to look at.

ARLIE: [*Now appears to lean on a bar rail.*] You git that haircut today, honey?

BENNIE: I just didn't want you givin your twenty dollars the warden gave you to the first pusher you come across.

[*Arlie laughs.*]

ARLENE: That's what you think I been waitin for?

ARLIE: Yeah! I heard ya. [*Is taken, quite roughly, by a GUARD, to a cell area.*]

BENNIE: But God Almighty, I hate to think what you'd done to the first ol bugger tried to make you in that bus station. You got grit, Arlie girl. I gotta credit you for that.

ARLIE: [*From the cell*] Officer!

BENNIE: The screamin you'd do. Wake the dead.

ARLENE: Uh-huh.

BENNIE: [*Proudly*] An there ain't nobody can beat you for throwin plates.

ARLIE: Are you gonna clean up this shit or do I have to sit here and look at it til I vomit?

BENNIE: Listen, ever prison in Alabama's usin plastic forks now on account of what you done.

ARLENE: You can quit talkin just anytime now.

ARLIE: Some life you got, fatso. Bringin me my dinner then wipin it off the walls. [*Laughs.*]

BENNIE: Some of them officers was pretty leery of you. Even the chaplain.

ARLENE: No he wasn't either.

BENNIE: Not me, though. You was just wild, that's all.

ARLENE: Animals is wild, not people. That's what he said.

ARLIE: [*Mocking*] Good behavior, good behavior. Shit.

BENNIE: Now what could that four-eyes chaplain know about wild?

[ARLENE *looks up sharply.*]

BENNIE: O.K. Not wild, then . . .

ARLIE: I kin git outta here anytime I want. [*Leaves the cell.*]

BENNIE: But you got grit, Arlie.

ARLENE: I have said for you to call me Arlene.

BENNIE: O.K. O.K.

ARLENE: Huh?

BENNIE: Don't git riled. You want me to call you Arlene, then Arlene it is. Yes, ma'am. Now [*Slapping the trunk*], where do you want this?

[*No response.*]

BENNIE: Arlene, I said, where do you want this trunk?

ARLENE: I don't care.

[BENNIE *starts to put it at the foot of the bed.* ARLENE *sees him.*]

ARLENE: No! [*Then calmer*] I seen it there too long.

[BENNIE *is understandably irritated.*]

ARLENE: Maybe over here. [*Points to a spot near the window.*] I could put a cloth on it and sit an look out the . . . [*She pulls the curtains apart, sees the bars on the window.*] What's these bars doin here?

BENNIE: [*Stops moving the trunk.*] I think they're to keep out burglars, you know. [*Sits on the trunk.*]

ARLENE: Yeah, I know.

ARLIE: [*Appearing on the catwalk, as if stopped during a break-in*] We ain't breakin in, cop, we're just admirin this beautiful window.

ARLENE: I don't want them there. Pull them out.

BENNIE: You can't go tearin up the place, Arlene. Landlord wouldn't like it.

ARLIE: [*To the unseen policeman*] Maybe I got a brick in my hand and maybe I don't.

BENNIE: Not one bit.

ARLIE: An I'm standin on this garbage can because I like to, all right?

ARLENE: I ain't gonna let no landlord tell me what to do. [*Fairly strong; walking back toward him*]

BENNIE: The landlord owns the building. You gotta do what he says or he'll throw you out right on your pretty little *be*hind. [*Gives her a familiar pat.*]

ARLENE: [*Slaps his hand away.*] You watch your mouth. I won't have no dirty talk.

ARLIE: Just shut the fuck up, pig! Go bust a wino or somethin. [*Returns to the cell.*]

ARLENE: Here, put the trunk over here.

BENNIE: What you got in here, anyhow? Rocks? Rocks from the rock pile? [*Carrying the trunk over to the spot she has picked*]

ARLENE: That ain't funny.

BENNIE: Oh sweetie, I didn't mean nuthin by that.

ARLENE: And I ain't your sweetie.

BENNIE: We really did have us a rock pile, you know, at the old Men's Prison, yes we did. And those boys, time they did nine or ten years carryin' rocks around, they were pret-ty mean, I'm here to tell you. And strong? God.

ARLENE: Well, what did you expect? [*Beginning to unpack the trunk*]

BENNIE: You're tellin me. It was dumb, I kept tellin the warden that. They coulda killed us all, easy, anytime, that outfit. Except, we did have the guns.

ARLENE: Uh-huh.

BENNIE: One old bastard sailed a throwin-rock right at me one day, woulda took my eye out if I hadn't turned around just then. Still got the scar, see? [*Reaches up to the back of his head.*]

ARLENE: You shoot him?

BENNIE: Nope. Somebody else did. I forget who. Hey! [*Walking over to the window*] These bars won't be so bad. Maybe you could get you some plants so's you don't even see them. Yeah, plants'd do it up just fine. Just fine.

ARLENE: [*Pulls a cheaply framed picture of Jesus out of the trunk.*] Chaplain give me this.

BENNIE: He got it for free, I bet.

ARLENE: Now, look here. That chaplain was good to me, so you can shut up about him.

BENNIE: Fine. Fine. [*Backing down*]

ARLENE: Here. [*Handing him the picture*] You might as well be useful 'fore you go.

BENNIE: Where you want it?

ARLENE: Don't matter.

BENNIE: Course it matters. Wouldn't want me puttin it inside the closet, would you? You gotta make decisions now, Arlene. Gotta decide things.

ARLENE: I don't care.

BENNIE: [*Insisting*] Arlene.

ARLENE: There. [*Pointing to a prominent position on the apartment wall, center*]

BENNIE: Yeah. Good place. See it first thing when you get up.

[ARLENE *lights a cigarette, as* ARLIE *retrieves a hidden lighter from the toilet in the cell.*]

ARLIE: There's ways ... gettin outta bars ...
[*Appears to light a fire in the cell, catching her blouse on fire too.*]

BENNIE: [*As* ARLIE *is lighting the fire*] This ol nail's pretty loose. I'll find something better to hang it with ... somewhere or other ...

ARLIE: [*Screams and the* DOCTOR *runs toward her, getting the attention of* EVANS, *a guard who has been goofing off on the catwalk.*] Let me outta here! There's a fuckin fire in here!
[DOCTOR *arrives at the cell, pats his pockets as if looking for the keys.*]

ARLIE: Officer!

DOCTOR: Guard!
[GUARD *begins his run to the cell.*]

ARLIE: It's burnin me!

DOCTOR: Hurry!

GUARD: I'm comin! I'm comin!

DOCTOR: What the hell were you—

GUARD: Come on, come on— [*Fumbling for the right key*]

DOCTOR: For Chrissake!
[*Urgent.* GUARD *gets the door open, they rush in.*]

DOCTOR: [*Wrestling* ARLIE *to the ground, opens his bag.*] Lay still, dammit.
[ARLIE *collapses,* DOCTOR *may appear to give an injection.*]

DOCTOR: Ow! [*Grabbing his hand*]

GUARD: [*Lifting* ARLIE *up to the bed*] Get bit, Doc?

DOCTOR: You going to let her burn this place down before you start payin attention up there?

GUARD: [*Walks to the toilet, feels under the rim.*] Uh-huh.

BENNIE: There, that what you had in mind? [*the picture*]

ARLENE: Yeah, thanks.

GUARD: She musta had them matches hid right here.

BENNIE: [*Who has hung the picture and is now staring at it*] How you think he kept his beard trimmed all nice?

ARLENE: [*Preoccupied with unloading the trunk*] Who?

BENNIE: [*Pointing to the picture*] Jesus.

DOCTOR: [*Quite stern*] I'll have to report you for this.

ARLENE: I don't know.

DOCTOR: That injection should hold her. I'll check back later. [*Leaves.*]

GUARD: [*Walking over to the bed*] Report me, my ass. We got cells don't have potties, Holsclaw. [*Begins to search her and the bed, handling her very roughly.*] So where is it now? Got it up your pookie, I bet. Oh, that'd be good. Doc comin back an me with my fingers up your. . . . Roll over. . . . Don't weigh hardly nuthin, do you, dollie?

BENNIE: Never seen him without a moustache either.

ARLENE: Huh?

BENNIE: The picture.

GUARD: Aw now . . . [*Finding the lighter under the mattress*] That wasn't hard at all. Don't you know bout hide an seek, Arlie, girl? Gonna hide somethin, hide it where it's fun to find it. [*Standing up, going to the door*] Crazy fuckin someday-we-ain't-gonna-come-save-you bitch!

BENNIE: Well, Arlie girl. . .

[GUARD *slams cell door and leaves.*]

BENNIE: That ol trunk's bout as empty as my belly.

ARLENE: You have been talkin bout your belly ever since we left this mornin.

BENNIE: You hungry? Them hot dogs we had give out around Nashville.

ARLENE: No. Not really.

BENNIE: You gotta eat, Arlene.

ARLENE: Says who?

BENNIE: [*Laughs, this is a familiar response.*] How bout I pick us up some chicken, give you time to clean yourself up. We'll have a nice little dinner, just the two of us.

ARLENE: I git sick if I eat this late. Besides, I'm tired.

BENNIE: You'll feel better soon's you git somethin on your

stomach. Like I always said, "Can't plow less'n you feed the mule."

ARLENE: I ain't never heard you say that.

BENNIE: There's lots you don't know about me, Arlene. You been seein me ever day, but you ain't been payin attention. You'll get to like me now we're out.

ARLENE: You . . . was always out.

BENNIE: Yes sir, I'm gonna like being retired. I kin tell already. An I can take care of you, like I been, only now—

ARLENE: [Interrupting] You tol me you was jus takin a vacation.

BENNIE: I was gonna tell you.

ARLENE: You had some time off an nuthin to do . . .

BENNIE: Figured you knew already.

ARLENE: You said you ain't never seen Kentucky like you always wanted to. Now you tell me you done quit at the prison? [Increasingly angry]

BENNIE: They wouldn't let me drive you up here if I was still on the payroll, you know. Rules, against the rules. Coulda got me in big trouble doin that.

ARLENE: You ain't goin back to Pine Ridge?

BENNIE: Nope.

ARLENE: An you drove me all the way up here plannin to stay here?

BENNIE: I was thinkin on it.

ARLENE: Well what are you gonna do?

BENNIE: [Not positive, just a possibility] Hardware.

ARLENE: Sell guns?

BENNIE: [Laughs and shakes his head "no."] Nails. Always wanted to. Some little store with bins and barrels full of nails and screws. Count em out. Put em in little sacks.

ARLENE: I don't need nobody hangin around remindin me where I been.

BENNIE: We had us a good time drivin up here, didn't we? You throwin that tomato outta the car . . . hit that

No Litterin sign square in the middle. [*Grabs her arm as if to feel the muscle.*] Good arm you got.

ARLENE: [*Pulling away sharply*] Don't you go grabbin me.

BENNIE: Listen, you take off them clothes and have yourself a nice hot bath. [*Heading for the bathroom*] See, I'll start the water. And me, I'll go get us some chicken. [*Coming out of the bathroom*] You like slaw or potato salad?

ARLENE: Don't matter.

BENNIE: [*Asking her to decide*], Arlene . . .

ARLENE: Slaw.

BENNIE: One big bucket of slaw comin right up. An extra rolls. You have a nice bath, now, you hear? I'll take my time so's you don't have to hurry fixin yourself up.

ARLENE: I ain't gonna do no fixin.

BENNIE: [*A knowing smile*] I know how you gals are when you get in the tub. You got any bubbles?

ARLENE: What?

BENNIE: Bubbles. You know, stuff to make bubbles with . . . bubble bath.

ARLENE: I thought you was goin.

BENNIE: Right. Right. Goin right now.

[BENNIE *leaves, locking the door behind him. He has left his hat on the bed.*]

[ARLENE *checks the stove and refrigerator, then goes into the bathroom when noted.*]

GUARD: [*Opening the cell door, carrying a plastic dinner carton*] Got your grub, girlie.

ARLIE: Get out!

GUARD: Can't. Doc says you gotta take the sun today.

ARLIE: You take it! I ain't hungry.

[GUARD *and* ARLIE *begin walk to the downstage table area.*]

GUARD: You gotta eat, Arlie.

ARLIE: Says who?

GUARD: Says me. Says the warden. Says the Department of Corrections. Brung you two rolls.

ARLIE: And you know what you can do with your—

GUARD: Stuff em in your bra, why don't you?

ARLIE: Ain't you got somebody to go beat up somewhere?

GUARD: Gotta see you get fattened up.

ARLIE: What do you care?

[ARLENE *goes into the bathroom.*]

GUARD: Oh, we care all right. [*Setting the food down on the table*] Got us a two-way mirror in the shower room. [*She looks up, hostile.*]

GUARD: And you don't know which one it is, do you? [*He forces her onto the seat.*] Yes, ma'am. Eat. [*Pointing to the food*] We sure do care if you go gittin too skinny. [*Walks away, folding his arms and standing watching her, her anger building, despite her hunger.*] Yes, ma'am. We care a hog-lickin lot.

ARLIE: Sons a bitches!

[*Throws the whole carton at him, yelling and running toward him. He catches her and carries her offstage.* MOTHER's *knock is heard on the apartment door.*]

MOTHER: Arlie? Arlie girl you in there?

[ARLENE *walks out of the bathroom, stands still, looking at the door.* ARLIE *hears the knock at the same time and slips into the apartment and over to the bed, putting the pillow between her legs and holding the yellow teddy bear* ARLENE *has unpacked.*]

MOTHER: [*Knocking louder*] Arlie?

ARLIE: [*Pulling herself up weakly on one elbow; speaking with the voice of a very young child*] Mama? Mama? [ARLENE *walks slowly toward the door.*]

MOTHER: [*Now pulling the doorknob from the outside, angry that the door is locked*] Arlie? I know you're in there.

ARLIE: I can't git up, Mama. [*Hands between her legs*] My legs is hurt.

MOTHER: What's takin you so long?

ARLENE: [*Smoothing out her dress*] Yeah, I'm comin.

[*Puts* BENNIE's *hat out of sight under the bed.*] Hold on.

MOTHER: I brung you some stuff but I ain't gonna stand here all night.

[ARLENE *opens the door and stands back.* MOTHER *looks strong but badly worn. She is wearing her cab-driver's uniform and is carrying a plastic laundry basket stuffed with cleaning fluids, towels, bug spray, etc.*]

ARLENE: I didn't know if you'd come.

MOTHER: Ain't I always?

ARLENE: How are you?

[*Moves as if to hug her.* MOTHER *stands still,* ARLENE *backs off.*]

MOTHER: Bout the same. [*Walking into the room*]

ARLENE: I'm glad to see you.

MOTHER: [*Not looking at* ARLENE] You look tired.

ARLENE: It was a long drive.

MOTHER: [*Putting the laundry basket on the trunk*] Didn't fatten you up none, I see. [*Walks around the room, looking the place over.*] You always was too skinny.

[ARLENE *straightens her clothes again.*]

MOTHER: Shoulda beat you like your daddy said. Make you eat.

ARLIE: Nobody done this to me, Mama. [*Protesting, in pain*] No! No!

MOTHER: He weren't a mean man, though, your daddy.

ARLIE: Was . . . [*Quickly*] my bike. My bike hurt me. The seat bumped me.

MOTHER: You remember that black chewing gum he got you when you were sick?

ARLENE: I remember he beat up on you.

MOTHER: Yeah, [*Proudly*] and he was real sorry a coupla times. [*Looking in the closet*] Filthy dirty. Hey!

[*Slamming the closet door,* ARLENE *jumps at the noise.*]

MOTHER: I brung you all kinda stuff. Just like Candy not

leavin you nuthin. [*Walking back to the basket*] Some
kids I got.

ARLIE: [*Curling up into a ball*] No, Mama, don't touch it.
It'll git well. It git well before.

ARLENE: Where is Candy?

MOTHER: You got her place so what do you care? I got
her outta my house so whatta I care? This'll be a good
place for you.

ARLENE: [*Going to the window*] Wish there was a yard,
here.

MOTHER: [*Beginning to empty the basket*] Nice things,
see? Bet you ain't had no colored towels where you
been.

ARLENE: No.

MOTHER: [*Putting some things away in cabinets*] No
place like home. Got that up on the kitchen wall now.

ARLIE: I don't want no tea, Mama.

ARLENE: Yeah?

MOTHER: [*Repeating* ARLENE's *answers*] No. . . . Yeah? . . .
You forgit how to talk? I ain't gonna be here all that
long. Least you can talk to me while I'm here.

ARLENE: You ever git that swing you wanted?

MOTHER: Dish towels, an see here? June sent along this
teapot. You drink tea, Arlie?

ARLENE: No.

MOTHER: June's havin another baby. Don't know when
to quit, that girl. Course, I ain't one to talk. [*Starting
to pick up trash on the floors, etc.*]

ARLENE: Have you seen Joey?

ARLIE: I'm tellin you the truth.

MOTHER: An Ray . . .

ARLIE: Daddy didn't do nuthin to me.

MOTHER: Ray ain't had a day of luck in his life.

ARLIE: Ask him. He saw me fall on my bike.

MOTHER: Least bein locked up now, he'll keep off June
til the baby gits here.

ARLENE: Have you seen Joey?

MOTHER: Your daddy ain't doin too good right now. Man's been dyin for ten years, to hear him tell it. You'd think he'd git tired of it an jus go ahead . . . pass on.

ARLENE: Mother . . . [*Wanting an answer*]

MOTHER: Yeah, I seen im. Bout two years ago. Got your stringy hair.

ARLENE: You got a picture?

MOTHER: You was right to give him up. Foster homes is good for some kids.

ARLIE: Where's my Joey-bear? Yellow Joey-bear? Mama?

ARLENE: How'd you see him?

MOTHER: I was down at Detention Center pickin up Pete. [*Beginning her serious cleaning now*]

ARLENE: How is he? [*Less than interested*]

MOTHER: I could be workin at the Detention Center I been there so much. All I gotta do's have somethin big goin on an I git a call to come after one of you. Can't jus have kids, no, gotta be pickin em up all over town.

ARLENE: You was just tellin me . . .

MOTHER: Pete is taller, that's all.

ARLENE: You was just tellin me how you saw Joey.

MOTHER: I'm comin back in the cab an I see him waitin for the bus.

ARLENE: What'd he say?

MOTHER: Oh, I didn't stop.

[ARLENE *looks up quickly, hurt and angry.*]

MOTHER: If the kid don't even know you, Arlie, he sure ain't gonna know who I am.

ARLENE: How come he couldn't stay at Shirley's?

MOTHER: Cause Shirley never was crazy about washin more diapers. She's the only smart kid I got. Anyway, social worker only put him there til she could find him a foster home.

ARLENE: But I coulda seen him.

MOTHER: Thatta been trouble, him bein in the family. Kid wouldn't have known who to listen to, Shirley or you.

ARLENE: But I'm his mother.

MOTHER: [*Interrupting*] See, now you don't have to be worryin about him. No kids, no worryin.

ARLENE: He just had his birthday, you know.

ARLIE: Don't let Daddy come in here, Mama. Just you an me. Mama?

ARLENE: When I git workin, I'll git a nice rug for this place. He could come live here with me.

MOTHER: Fat chance.

ARLENE: I done my time.

MOTHER: You never really got attached to him anyway.

ARLENE: How do you know that? [*Furious*]

MOTHER: Now don't you go getting het up. I'm tellin you—

ARLENE: But—

MOTHER: Kids need rules to go by and he'll get em over there.

ARLIE: No, Daddy! I didn't tell her nuthin. I didn't! I didn't! [*Screaming, gets up from the bed, terrified.*]

MOTHER: Here, help me with these sheets. [*Hands* ARLENE *the sheets from the laundry basket.*] Even got you a spread. Kinda goes with them curtains. [ARLENE *is silent.*] You ain't thanked me, Arlie girl.

ARLENE: [*Going to the other side of the bed*] They don't call me Arlie no more. It's Arlene now.

[ARLENE *and* MOTHER *make up the bed.*

ARLIE *jumps up, looks around and goes over to* MOTHER's *purse. She looks through it hurriedly and pulls out the wallet. She takes some money and runs downstage left where she is caught by a* SCHOOL PRINCIPAL.]

SCHOOL PRINCIPAL: Arlie? You're in an awfully big hurry for such a little girl. [*Brushes at* ARLIE's *hair.*] That is you under all that hair, isn't it?

[ARLIE *resists this gesture.*]

PRINCIPAL: Now, you can watch where you're going.

ARLIE: Gotta git home.

PRINCIPAL: But school isn't over for another three hours.

And there's peanut butter and chili today. [*As if this mattered*]

ARLIE: Ain't hungry. [*Struggling free*]

PRINCIPAL: [*Now sees* ARLIE's *hands clenched behind her back.*] What do we have in our hands, Arlie? [*Sticky sweet over suspicion*]

ARLIE: Nuthin.

PRINCIPAL: Let me see your hands, Arlie. Open up your hands. [*Expecting the worst*]

ARLIE: [*Bringing hands around in front, opening them, showing crumpled dollars*] It's my money. I earned it.

PRINCIPAL: [*Taking the money*] And how did we earn this money?

ARLIE: Doin things.

PRINCIPAL: What kind of things?

ARLIE: For my daddy.

PRINCIPAL: Well, we'll see about that. You'll have to come with me.

ARLIE: No. [*Resisting as* PRINCIPAL *pulls her*]

PRINCIPAL: Your mother was right after all. She said put you in a special school. [*Quickly*] No, what she said was put you away somewhere and I said, No, she's too young, well I was wrong. I have four hundred other children to take care of here and what have I been doing? Breaking up your fights, talking to your truant officer and washing your writing off the bathroom wall. Well, I've had enough. You've made your choice. You *want* out of regular school and you're going to *get* out of regular school.

ARLIE: [*Becoming more violent*] You can't make me go nowhere, bitch!

PRINCIPAL: [*Backing off in cold anger*] I'm not making you go. You've earned it. You've worked hard for this, well, they're used to your type over there. They'll know exactly what to do with you.

[PRINCIPAL *stalks off, leaving* ARLIE *alone.*]

MOTHER: [*Smoothing out the spread*] Spread ain't new, but it don't look so bad. Think we got it right after we

got you. No, I remember now. I was pregnant with you
an been real sick the whole time.

[ARLENE *lights a cigarette,* MOTHER *takes one,* ARLENE
retrieves the pack quickly.]

MOTHER: Your daddy brung me home this big bowl of
chili an some jelly doughnuts. Some fare from the air-
port give him a big tip. Anyway, I'd been eatin peanut
brittle all day, only thing that tasted any good. Then in
he come with this chili an no sooner'n I got in bed I
thrown up all over everwhere. Lucky I didn't throw
you up, Arlie girl. Anyhow, that's how come us to get
a new spread. This one here. [*Sits on the bed.*]

ARLENE: You drivin the cab any?

MOTHER: Any? Your daddy ain't drove it at all a long time
now. Six years, seven maybe.

ARLENE: You meet anybody nice?

MOTHER: Not any more. Mostly drivin old ladies to get
their shoes. Guess it got around the nursin homes I was
reliable. [*Sounds funny to her.*] You remember that
time I took you drivin with me that night after you been
in a fight an that soldier bought us a beer? Shitty place,
hole in the wall?

ARLENE: You made me wait in the car.

MOTHER: [*Standing up*] Think I'd take a child of mine
into a dump like that?

ARLENE: You went in.

MOTHER: Weren't no harm in it. [*Walking over for the
bug spray*] I didn't always look so bad, you know.

ARLENE: You was pretty.

MOTHER: [*Beginning to spray the floors*] You could look
better'n you do. Do somethin with your hair. I always
thought if you'd looked better you wouldn't have got
in so much trouble.

ARLENE: [*Pleased and curious*] Joey got my hair?

MOTHER: And skinny.

ARLENE: I took some beauty school at Pine Ridge.

MOTHER: Yeah, a beautician?

ARLENE: I don't guess so.

MOTHER: Said you was gonna work.

ARLENE: They got a law here. Ex-cons can't get a license.

MOTHER: Shoulda stayed in Alabama, then. Worked there.

ARLENE: They got a law there, too.

MOTHER: Then why'd they give you the trainin?

ARLENE: I don't know.

MOTHER: Maybe they thought it'd straighten you out.

ARLENE: Yeah.

MOTHER: But you are gonna work, right? [*Doesn't want another burden.*]

ARLENE: Yeah. Cookin maybe. Somethin that pays good.

MOTHER: You? Cook? [*Laughs.*]

ARLENE: I could learn it.

MOTHER: Your daddy ain't never forgive you for that bologna sandwich.

[ARLENE *laughs a little, finally enjoying a memory.*]

MOTHER: Oh, I wish I'd seen you spreadin that Colgate on that bread. He'd have smelled that toothpaste if he hadn't been so sloshed. Little snotty-nosed kid tryin to kill her daddy with a bologna sandwich. And him bein so pleased when you brung it to him . . . [*Laughing*]

ARLENE: [*Suddenly sober*] He beat me good.

MOTHER: Well, now, Arlie, you gotta admit you had it comin to you. [*Wiping tears from laughing*]

ARLENE: I guess.

MOTHER: You got a broom?

ARLENE: No.

MOTHER: Well, I got one in the cab I brung just in case. I can't leave it here, but I'll sweep up fore I go. [*Walking toward the door*] You jus rest til I git back. Won't find no work lookin the way you do.

[MOTHER *leaves,* ARLENE *finds some lipstick and a mirror in her purse, she makes an attempt to look better while* MOTHER *is gone.*]

ARLIE: [*Jumps up, as if talking to another kid.*] She is not skinny!

ARLENE: [*Looking at herself in the mirror*] I guess I could—

ARLIE: And she don't have to git them stinky permanents. Her hair just comes outta her head curly.

ARLENE: Some lipstick.

ARLIE: [*Serious*] She drives the cab to buy us stuff, cause we don't take no charity from nobody, cause we got money cause she earned it.

ARLENE: [*Closing the mirror, dejected, afraid* MOTHER *might be right*] But you're too skinny and you got stringy hair. [*Sitting on the floor*]

ARLIE: [*More angry*] She drives at night cause people needs rides at night. People goin to see their friends that are sick, or people's cars broken down and they gotta get to work at the ... nobody calls my mama a whore!

MOTHER: [*Coming back in with the broom*] If I'd known you were gonna sweep up with your butt, I wouldn't have got this broom. Get up! [*Sweeps at* ARLENE *to get her to move.*]

ARLIE: You're gonna take that back or I'm gonna rip out all your ugly hair and stuff it down your ugly throat.

ARLENE: [*Tugging at her own hair*] You still cut hair?

MOTHER: [*Noticing some spot on the floor*] Gonna take a razor blade to get out this paint.

ARLENE: Nail polish.

ARLIE: Wanna know what I know about your mama? She's dyin. Somethin's eatin up her insides piece by piece, only she don't want you to know it.

MOTHER: [*Continuing to sweep*] So, you're callin yourself Arlene, now?

ARLENE: Yes.

MOTHER: Don't want your girlie name no more?

ARLENE: Somethin like that.

MOTHER: They call you Arlene in prison?

ARLENE: Not at first when I was bein hateful. Just my number then.

MOTHER: You always been hateful.

[ARLENE *reaches for the broom.*]

MOTHER: I'll do it.

ARLENE: You kin rest.

MOTHER: Since when?

[ARLENE *backs off;* MOTHER *sweeping harder now.*]

MOTHER: I ain't hateful, how come I got so many hateful kids? Poor dumb-as-hell Pat, stealin them wigs, Candy screwin since day one, Pete cutting up ol Mac down at the grocery, June sellin dope like it was Girl Scout cookies, and you. . . . Thank God I can't remember it all.

ARLENE: Maybe I could come out on Sunday for . . . you still make that pot roast?

MOTHER: [*Now sweeping over by the picture of Jesus*] That your picture?

ARLENE: That chaplain give it to me.

MOTHER: The one give you your "new name."

ARLENE: Yes.

MOTHER: It's crooked. [*Doesn't straighten it.*]

ARLENE: I liked those potatoes with no skins. An that ketchup squirter we had, jus like in a real restaurant.

MOTHER: People that run them institutions now, they jus don't know how to teach kids right. Let em run around an get in more trouble. They should get you up at the crack of dawn an set you to scrubbin the floor. That's what kids need. Trainin. Hard work.

ARLENE: [*A clear request*] I'll probably git my Sundays off.

MOTHER: Sunday . . . is my day to clean house now.

[ARLENE *gets the message, finally walks over to straighten the picture.* MOTHER *now feels a little bad about this rejection, stops sweeping for a moment.*]

MOTHER: I woulda wrote you but I didn't have nuthin to say. An no money to send, so what's the use?

ARLENE: I made out.

MOTHER: They pay you for workin?

ARLENE: Bout three dollars a month.

MOTHER: How'd you make out on three dollars a month? [*Answers her own question.*] You do some favors?

ARLENE: [*Sitting down in the chair under the picture, a somewhat smug look*] You jus can't make it by yourself.

MOTHER: [*Pauses, suspicious, then contemptuous.*] You play, Arlie?

ARLENE: You don't know nuthin about that.

MOTHER: I hear things. Girls callin each other "mommy" an bringin things back from the canteen for their "husbands." Makes me sick. You got family, Arlie, what you want with that playin? Don't want nobody like that in my house.

ARLENE: You don't know what you're talkin about.

MOTHER: I still got two kids at home. Don't want no bad example. [*Not finishing the sweeping. Has all the dirt in one place, but doesn't get it up off the floor yet.*]

ARLENE: I could tell them . . . about things.

MOTHER: Like about that cabdriver. [*Vicious*]

ARLENE: Look, that was a long time ago. I wanna work, now, make somethin of myself. I learned to knit. People'll buy nice sweaters. Make some extra money.

MOTHER: We sure could use it.

ARLENE: An then if I have money, maybe they'd let me take Joey to the fair, buy him hot dogs and talk to him. Make sure he ain't foolin around.

MOTHER: What makes you think he'd listen to you? Alice, across the street? Her sister took care her kids while she was at Lexington. You think they pay any attention to her now? Ashamed, that's what. One of em told me his mother done died. Gone to see a friend and died there.

ARLENE: Be different with me and Joey.

MOTHER: He don't even know who you are, Arlie.

ARLENE: Arlene. [*She can't respond, this is all she can say.*]

MOTHER: You forgot already what you was like as a kid. At Waverly, tellin them lies about that campin trip we took, sayin your daddy made you watch while he an me . . . you know. I'd have killed you then if them social workers hadn't been watchin.

ARLENE: Yeah.

MOTHER: Didn't want them thinkin I weren't fit. Well, what do they know? Each time you'd get out of one of them places, you'd be actin worse than ever. Go right back to that junkie pimp Carl, sellin the stuff he steals, savin his ass from the police. He follow you home this time, too?

ARLENE: He's got four more years at Bricktown.

MOTHER: Glad to hear it. Here. . . . [*Handing her a bucket*] Water.

[ARLENE *fills up the bucket and* MOTHER *washes several dirty spots on the walls, floor and furniture.* ARLENE *knows better than to try to help. The* DOCTOR *walks downstage to find* ARLIE *for their counseling session.*]

DOCTOR: So you refuse to go to camp?

ARLIE: Now why'd I want to go to your fuckin camp? Camp's for babies. You can go shit in the woods if you want to, but I ain't goin.

DOCTOR: Oh, you're goin.

ARLIE: Wanna bet?

MOTHER: Arlie, I'm waitin. [*For the water*]

ARLIE: 'Sides, I'm waitin.

DOCTOR: Waiting for what?

ARLIE: For Carl to come git me.

DOCTOR: And who is Carl?

ARLIE: Jus some guy. We're goin to Alabama.

DOCTOR: You don't go til we say you can go.

ARLIE: Carl's got a car.

DOCTOR: Does he have a driver's license to go with it?

ARLIE: [*Enraged, impatient*] I'm goin now.

[*She stalks away, then backs up toward him again. He has information she wants.*]

DOCTOR: Hey!

ARLENE: June picked out a name for the baby?

MOTHER: Clara . . . or Clarence. Got it from this fancy shampoo she bought.

ARLIE: I don't feel good. I'm pregnant, you know.

DOCTOR: The test was negative.

ARLIE: Well, I should know, shouldn't I?

DOCTOR: No. You want to be pregnant, is that it?

ARLIE: I wouldn't mind. Kids need somebody to bring em up right.

DOCTOR: Raising children is a big responsibility, you know.

ARLIE: Yeah, I know it. I ain't dumb. Everybody always thinks I'm so dumb.

DOCTOR: You could learn if you wanted to. That's what the teachers are here for. •

ARLIE: Shit.

DOCTOR: Or so they say.

ARLIE: All they teach us is about geography. Why'd I need to know about Africa. Jungles and shit.

DOCTOR: They want you to know about other parts of the world.

ARLIE: Well, I ain't goin there so whatta I care?

DOCTOR: What's this about Cindy?

ARLIE: [*Hostile*] She told Mr. Dawson some lies about me.

DOCTOR: I bet.

ARLIE: She said I fuck my daddy for money.

DOCTOR: And what did you do when she said that?

ARLIE: What do you think I did? I beat the shit out of her.

DOCTOR: And that's a good way to work out your problem?

ARLIE: She ain't done it since. [*Proud*]

DOCTOR: She's been in traction, since.

ARLIE: So, whatta I care? She say it again, I'll do it again. Bitch!

ARLENE: [*Looking down at the dirt* MOTHER *is gathering on the floor*] I ain't got a can. Just leave it.

MOTHER: And have you sweep it under the bed after I

go? [*Wraps the dirt in a piece of newspaper and puts it in her laundry basket.*]

DOCTOR: [*Looking at his clipboard*] You're on unit cleanup this week.

ARLIE: I done it last week!

DOCTOR: Then you should remember what to do. The session is over. [*Getting up, walking away*] And stand up straight! And take off that hat!

[DOCTOR *and* ARLIE *go offstage as* MOTHER *finds* BEN-NIE's *hat.*]

MOTHER: This your hat?

ARLENE: No.

MOTHER: Guess Candy left it here.

ARLENE: Candy didn't leave nuthin. [*Then realizes this was a mistake.*]

MOTHER: Then whose is it?

[ARLENE *doesn't answer.*]

MOTHER: Do you know whose hat this is?

[ARLENE *turns away.*]

MOTHER: I'm askin you a question and I want an answer.

[ARLENE *turns her back to* MOTHER.]

MOTHER: Whose hat is this? You tell me right now, whose hat is this?

ARLENE: It's Bennie's.

MOTHER: And who's Bennie?

ARLENE: Guy drove me home from Pine Ridge. A guard.

MOTHER: [*Upset*] I knew it. You been screwin a goddamn guard. [*Throws the hat on the bed.*]

ARLENE: He jus drove me up here, that's all.

MOTHER: Sure.

ARLENE: I git sick on the bus.

MOTHER: You expect me to believe that?

ARLENE: I'm tellin you, he jus—

MOTHER: No man alive gonna drive a girl five hundred miles for nuthin.

ARLENE: He ain't never seen Kentucky.

MOTHER: It ain't Kentucky he wants to see.

ARLENE: He ain't gettin nuthin from me.

MOTHER: That's what you think.

ARLENE: He done some nice things for me at Pine Ridge. Gum, funny stories.

MOTHER: He'll be tellin stories all right, tellin his buddies where to find you.

ARLENE: He's gettin us some dinner right now.

MOTHER: And how're you gonna pay him? Huh? Tell me that.

ARLENE: I ain't like that no more.

MOTHER: Oh you ain't. I'm your mother. I know what you'll do.

ARLENE: I tell you I ain't.

MOTHER: I knew it. Well, when you got another bastard in you, don't come cryin to me, cause I done told you.

ARLENE: Don't worry.

MOTHER: An I'm gettin myself outta here fore your boyfriend comes back.

ARLENE: He ain't my boyfriend. [*Increasing anger*]

MOTHER: I been a lotta things, but I ain't dumb, Arlene. ["ARLENE" *is mocking.*]

ARLENE: I didn't say you was. [*Beginning to know how this is going to turn out*]

MOTHER: Oh no? You lied to me!

ARLENE: How?

MOTHER: You took my spread without even sayin thank you. [*Not an answer. Just going on with the fury.*] You're hintin at comin to my hosue for pot roast just like nuthin ever happened, an all the time you're hidin a goddamn guard under your bed. [*Furious*] Uh-huh.

ARLENE: [*Quietly*] Mama?

MOTHER: [*Cold, fierce*] What?

ARLENE: What kind of meat makes a pot roast?

MOTHER: A roast makes a pot roast. Buy a roast. Shoulder, chuck. . . .

ARLENE: Are you comin back?

MOTHER: You ain't got no need for me.

ARLENE: I gotta ask you to come see me?

MOTHER: I come tonight, didn't I, an nobody asked me?

ARLENE: Jus forget it.

MOTHER: [*Getting her things together now, ready to go*] An if I hadn't told them about this apartment, you wouldn't be out at all, how bout that!

ARLENE: [*Stronger*] Forget it!

MOTHER: Don't you go talkin to me that way. You remember who I am. I'm the one took you back after all you done all them years. I brung you that teapot. I scrubbed your place. You remember that when you talk to me.

ARLENE: Sure.

MOTHER: Uh-huh. [*Now goes to the bed, rips off the spread and stuffs it in her basket.*] I knowed I shouldn't have come. You ain't changed a bit.

ARLENE: Same hateful brat, right? [*Back to* MOTHER.]

MOTHER: Same hateful brat. Right. [*Arms full, heading for the door*]

ARLENE: [*Rushing toward her*] Mama . . .

MOTHER: Don't you touch me.

[MOTHER *leaves*.

ARLENE *stares out the door, stunned and hurt; finally, she slams the door and turns back into the room.*]

ARLENE: No! Don't you touch Mama, Arlie.

RONNIE: [*A fellow juvenile offender, runs across the cat-walk, waving a necklace and being chased by* ARLIE.] Arlie got a boyfriend, Arlie got a boyfriend. [*Throws the necklace downstage.*] Whoo!

ARLIE: [*Chasing him*] Ronnie, you ugly mother, I'll smash your fuckin—

ARLENE: You might steal all— [*Getting more angry*]

RONNIE: [*Running down the stairs*] Arlie got a boyfriend—

ARLIE: Gimme that necklace or I'll—

ARLENE: . . . or eat all Mama's precious pot roast . . .

RONNIE: [*As they wrestle on the downstage apron*] You'll tell the doctor on me? And get your private room back? [*Laughing*]

ARLENE: [*Cold and hostile*] No, don't touch Mama, Arlie. Cause you might slit Mama's throat. [*Goes into the bathroom.*]

ARLIE: You wanna swallow all them dirty teeth?

RONNIE: Tell me who give it to you.

ARLIE: No, you tell me where it's at.

RONNIE: [*Breaks away, pushing* ARLIE *in the opposite direction, runs for the necklace.*] It's right here. [*Drops it down his pants.*] Come an git it.

ARLIE: Oh now, that was really ignorant, you stupid pig.

RONNIE: [*Backing away, daring her*] Just reach right in. First come, first served.

ARLIE: Now, how you gonna pee after I throw your weenie over the fence?

RONNIE: You ain't gonna do that, girl. You gonna fall in love.

[*She turns vicious, pins him down, attacking. This is no longer play. He screams.* DOCTOR *appears on the catwalk.*]

DOCTOR: Arlie! [*Heads down the stairs to stop this.*]

CARL: [*From outside the apartment door.*] Arlie!

DOCTOR: Arlie!

ARLIE: Stupid, ugly—

RONNIE: Help!

[ARLIE *runs off, hides downstage left.*]

DOCTOR: That's three more weeks of isolation, Arlie. [*Bending down to* RONNIE] You all right? Can you walk?

RONNIE: [*Looking back to* ARLIE *as he gets up in great pain.*] She was tryin to kill me.

DOCTOR: Yeah. Easy now. You should've known, Ronnie.

ARLIE: [*Yelling at* RONNIE] You'll get yours, crybaby.

CARL: Arlie . . .

ARLIE: Yeah, I'm comin!

CARL: Bad-lookin dude says move your ass an open up this here door, girl.

[ARLENE *does not come out of the bathroom.* CARL *twists the door knob violently, then kicks in the door*

and walks in. CARL *is thin and cheaply dressed.* CARL's
*walk and manner are imitative of black pimps, but he
can't quite carry it off.*]

CARL: Where you at, Mama?

ARLENE: Carl?

CARL: Who else? You 'spectin Leroy Brown?

ARLENE: I'm takin a bath!

CARL: [*Walking toward the bathroom*] I like my ladies
clean. Matter of professional pride.

ARLENE: Don't come in here.

CARL: [*Mocking her tone*] Don't come in here. I seen it
all before, girl.

ARLENE: Hold your horses. I'm gittin out. Sit down or
somethin.

CARL: [*Talking loud enough for her to hear him through
the door*] Ain't got the time. [*Opens her purse, then
searches the trunk.*] Jus come by to tell you it's tomorrow. We be takin our feet to the New York street. [*As
though she will be pleased*] No more fuckin around
with these jiveass southern turkeys. We're goin to the
big city, baby. Get you some red shades and some red
shorts an the johns'll be linin up fore we hit town. Four
tricks a night. How's that sound? No use wearin out
that cute ass you got. Way I hear it, only way to git
busted up there's be stupid, an I ain't lived this long
bein stupid.

ARLENE: [*Coming out of the bathroom wearing a towel*]
That's exactly how you lived your whole life—bein stupid.

CARL: Arlie . . . [*Moving in on her*] Be sweet, sugar.

ARLENE: Still got your curls.

CARL: [*Trying to hug her*] You're lookin O.K. yourself.

ARLENE: Oh, Carl. [*Noticing the damage to the door;
breaking away from any closeness he might try to
force*]

CARL: [*Amused*] Bent up your door some.

ARLENE: How come you're out?

CARL: Sweetheart, you done broke out once, been nabbed

and sent to Pine Ridge and got yourself paroled since
I been in. I got a right to a little free time too, ain't that
right.

ARLENE: You escape?

CARL: Am I standin here or am I standin here? They been
fuckin with you, I can tell.

ARLENE: They gonna catch you.

CARL: [*Going to the window*] Not where we're going. Not
a chance.

ARLENE: Where you goin they won't git you?

CARL: Remember that green hat you picked out for me
down in Birmingham? Well, I ain't ever wore it yet,
but I kin wear it in New York cause New York's where
you wear just what you feel like. One guy tol me he
saw this dude wearin a whole ring of feathers roun his
leg, right here [*Grabs his leg above the knee.*] an he
weren't in no circus nor no Indian neither.

ARLENE: I ain't seen you since Birmingham. How come
you think I wanna see you now?

ARLIE: [*Coming up from under the table to confront
CARL*] Carl, I ain't goin with that dude, he's weird.
[*Pointing as if there is a trick waiting*]

CARL: Cause we gotta go collect the johns' money, that's
"how come."

ARLIE: I don't need you pimpin for me.

ARLENE: I'm gonna work.

CARL: Work?

ARLENE: Yeah.

CARL: What's this "work"?

ARLIE: You always sendin me to them ol' droolers . . .

CARL: You kin do two things, girl . . .

ARLIE: They slobberin all over me . . .

CARL: Breakin out an hookin.

ARLIE: They tyin me to the bed!

ARLENE: I mean real work.

ARLIE: [*Now screaming, gets further away from him*] I
could git killed workin for you. Some sicko, some crazy
drunk . . .

[*Goes offstage, enters the cell sometime before* BENNIE's *entrance.*]

CARL: You forget, we seen it all on TV in the dayroom, you bustin outta Lakewood like that. Fakin that palsy fit, then beatin that guard half to death with his own key ring. Whoo-ee! Then that spree you went on ... stoppin at that fillin station for some cash, then kidnappin the old dude pumpin the gas.

ARLENE: Yeah.

CARL: Then that cabdriver comes outta the bathroom an tries to mess with you and you shoots him with his own piece. [*Fires an imaginary pistol.*] That there's nice work, Mama. [*Going over to her, putting his arms around her*]

ARLENE: That gun ... it went off, Carl.

CARL: [*Getting more determined with his affection*] That's what guns do, doll. They go off.

BENNIE'S VOICE: [*From outside*] Arlene? Arlene?

CARL: Arlene? [*Jumping up*] Well, la de da.

[BENNIE *opens the door, carrying the chicken dinners. He is confused seeing* ARLENE *wearing a towel and talking to* CARL.]

ARLENE: Bennie, this here's Carl.

CARL: You're interruptin, jack. Me and Arlie got business.

BENNIE: She's callin herself Arlene.

CARL: I call my ladies what I feel like, chicken man, an you call yourself "gone."

BENNIE: I don't take orders from you.

CARL: Well, you been takin orders from somebody, or did you git them duds at the army surplus store.

ARLENE: Bennie brung me home from Pine Ridge, Carl.

CARL: [*Walking toward him*] Oh, it's a guard now, is it? That chicken break out or what? [*Grabs the chicken.*]

BENNIE: I don't know what you're doin here, but—

CARL: What you gonna do about it, huh? Lock me up in the toilet? You an who else, Batman?

BENNIE: [*Taking the chicken back, walking calmly to the counter*] Watch your mouth, punk. [*Condescending.*

Doesn't want a fight, for ARLENE's *sake, but doesn't want to appear threatened either.*]

CARL: [*Kicks a chair toward* BENNIE.] Punk!

ARLENE: [*Trying to stop this*] I'm hungry.

BENNIE: You heard her, she's hungry.

CARL: [*Vicious*] Shut up! [*Mocking*] Ossifer.

BENNIE: Arlene, tell this guy if he knows what's good for him . . .

CARL: [*Walking to the counter where* BENNIE *has left the chicken*] Why don't you write me a parkin ticket? [*Shoves the chicken on the floor.*] Don't fuck with me, Dad. It ain't healthy.

BENNIE: [*Pauses, a real standoff. Finally, bends down and picks up the chicken.*] You ain't worth dirtyin my hands. [CARL *walks by him, laughing.*]

CARL: Hey, Arlie. I got some dude to see. [*For* BENNIE's *benefit as he struts to the door*] What I need with another beat up guard? All that blood, jus ugly up my threads. [*Very sarcastic*] Bye y'all. [*Turns back quickly at the door, stopping* BENNIE *who was following him.*] You really oughta shine them shoes, man. [*Vindictive laugh, slams the door in* BENNIE's *face.*]

BENNIE: [*Relieved, trying to change the atmosphere*] Well, how bout if we eat? You'll catch your death dressed like that.

ARLENE: Turn around then.

[ARLENE *gets a shabby housecoat from the closet. She puts it on over the towel, buttons it up, then pulls the towel out from under it. This has the look of a prison ritual.*]

BENNIE: [*As she is dressing*] Your parole officer's gonna tell you to keep away from guys like that . . . for your own good, you know. Those types, just like the suckers on my tomatoes back home. Take everything right outta you. Gotta pull em off, Arlie . . . uh . . . Arlene.

ARLENE: Now, I'm decent now.

BENNIE: You hear what I said?

ARLENE: I told him that. That's exactly what I did tell him. [*Going to the bathroom for her hairbrush*]

BENNIE: Who was that anyhow? [*Sits down on the bed, opens up the chicken.*]

ARLENE: [*From the bathroom*] Long time ago, me an Carl took a trip together.

BENNIE: When you was a kid, you mean?

ARLENE: I was at this place for kids.

BENNIE: And Carl was there?

ARLENE: No, he picked me up an we went to Alabama. There was this wreck an all. I ended up at Lakewood for forgery. It was him that done it. Got me pregnant, too.

BENNIE: That was Joey's father?

ARLENE: Yeah, but he don't know that. [*Sits down.*]

BENNIE: Just as well. Guys like that, don't know what they'd do.

ARLENE: Mother was here while ago. Says she's seen Joey. [*Taking a napkin from* BENNIE]

BENNIE: Wish I had a kid. Life ain't, well, complete, without no kids to play ball with an take fishin. Dorrie, though, she had them backaches an that neuralgia, day I married her to the day she died. Good woman though. No drinkin, no card playin, real sweet voice. . . . What was the song she used to sing? . . . Oh, yeah . . .

ARLENE: She says Joey's a real good-lookin kid.

BENNIE: Well, his mom ain't bad.

ARLENE: At Lakewood, they tried to git me to have an abortion.

BENNIE: They was just thinkin of you, Arlene.

ARLENE: I told em I'd kill myself if they done that. I would have too. [*Matter-of-fact, no self-pity*]

BENNIE: But they took him away after he was born.

ARLENE: Yeah.

[BENNIE *waits, knowing she is about to say more.*]

ARLENE: An I guess I went crazy after that. Thought if I could jus git out an find him . . .

BENNIE: I don't remember any of that on the TV.

ARLENE: No.

BENNIE: Just remember you smilin at the cameras, yellin how you tol that cabdriver not to touch you.

ARLENE: I never seen his cab. [*Now forces herself to begin to eat.*]

ARLIE: [*In the cell, holding a pillow and singing*] Rock-a-bye baby, on the tree top, when the wind blows, the cradle will . . . [*Not remembering*] cradle will . . . [*Now talking*] What you gonna be when you grow up, pretty boy baby? You gonna be a doctor? You gonna give people medicine an take out they. . . . No, don't be no doctor . . . be . . . be a preacher . . . sayin Our Father who is in Heaven . . . Heaven, that's where people go when they dies, when doctors can't save em or somebody kills em fore they even git a chance to. . . . No, don't be no preacher neither. . . . Be . . . go to school an learn good [*Tone begins to change*] so you kin . . . make everbody else feel so stupid all the time. Best thing you to be is stay a baby cause nobody beats up on babies or puts them. . . . [*Much more quiet*] That ain't true, baby. People is mean to babies, so you stay right here with me so nobody kin get you an make you cry an they lay one finger on you [*Hostile*] an I'll beat the screamin shit right out of em. They even blow on you an I'll kill em.

[BENNIE *and* ARLENE *have finished their dinner.* BENNIE *puts one carton of slaw in the refrigerator, then picks up all the paper, making a garbage bag out of one of the sacks.*]

BENNIE: Ain't got a can, I guess. Jus use this ol sack for now.

ARLENE: I ain't never emptyin another garbage can.

BENNIE: Yeah, I reckon you know how by now. [*Yawns.*] You bout ready for bed?

ARLENE: [*Stands up.*] I spose.

BENNIE: [*Stretches.*] Little tired myself.

ARLENE: Thanks for the chicken. [*Dusting the crumbs off the bed*]

BENNIE: You're right welcome. You look beat. How bout I rub your back. [*Grabs her shoulders.*]

ARLENE: [*Pulling away*] No. [*Walking to the sink*] You go on now.

BENNIE: Oh come on. [*Wiping his hands on his pants*] I ain't all that tired.

ARLENE: *I'm* tired.

BENNIE: Well, see then, a back rub is just what the doctor ordered.

ARLENE: No. I don't . . . [*Pulling away*]

BENNIE: [*Grabs her shoulders and turns her around, sits her down hard on the trunk, starts rubbing her back and neck.*] Muscles git real tight like, right in here.

ARLENE: You're hurtin me.

BENNIE: Has to hurt a little or it won't do no good.

ARLENE: [*Jumps, he has hurt her.*] Oh, stop it! [*Slips away from him and out into the room. She is frightened.*]

BENNIE: [*Smiling, coming after her, toward the bed*] Be lot nicer if you was layin down. Wouldn't hurt as much.

ARLENE: Now, I ain't gonna start yellin. I'm jus tellin you to go.

BENNIE: [*Straightens up as though he's going to cooperate.*] O.K. then. I'll jus git my hat. [*He reaches for the hat, then turns quickly, grabs her and throws her down on the bed. He starts rubbing again.*] Now, you just relax. Don't go bein scared of me.

ARLENE: You ain't gettin nuthin from me.

BENNIE: I don't want nuthin, honey. Jus tryin to help you sleep.

ARLENE: [*Struggling*] Don't you call me honey.

BENNIE: [*Stops rubbing, but keeps one hand on her back. Rubs her hair with his free hand.*] See? Don't that feel better?

ARLENE: Let me up.

BENNIE: Why, I ain't holdin you down. [*So innocent*]

ARLENE: Then let me up.

BENNIE: [*Takes hands off.*] O.K. Git up.

ARLENE: [*Turns over slowly, begins to lift herself up on her elbows.* BENNIE *puts one hand on her leg.*] Move your hand.

BENNIE: [ARLENE *gets up, moves across the room.*] I'd be happy to stay here with you tonight. Make sure you'll be all right. You ain't spent a night by yourself for a long time.

ARLENE: I remember how.

BENNIE: Well how you gonna git up? You got a alarm?

ARLENE: It ain't all that hard.

BENNIE: [*Puts one hand in his pocket, leers a little*] Oh yeah it is. [*Walks toward her again*] Gimme a kiss. Then I'll go.

ARLENE: You stay away from me. [*Edging along the counter, seeing she's trapped*]

BENNIE: [*Reaches for her, clamping her hands behind her, pressing up against her.*] Now what's it going to hurt you to give me a little ol kiss?

ARLENE: Git out! I said git out! [*Struggling*]

BENNIE: You don't want me to go. You're jus beginning to git interested. Your ol girlie temper's flarin up. I like that in a woman.

ARLENE: Yeah, you'd love it if I'd swat you one. [*Getting away from him*]

BENNIE: I been hit by you before. I kin take anything you got.

ARLENE: I could mess you up good.

BENNIE: Now, Arlie. You ain't had a man in a long time. And the ones you had been no-count.

ARLENE: Git out! [*Slaps him. He returns the slap.*]

BENNIE: [*Moving in*] Ain't natural goin without it too long. Young thing like you. Git all shriveled up.

ARLENE: [ARLIE *turning on, now*] All right, you sunuva-bitch, you asked for it! [*Goes into a violent rage, hitting and kicking him.*]

BENNIE: [*Overpowering her capably, prison-guard style*] Little outta practice, ain't you? [*Amused*]

ARLENE: [*Screaming*] I'll kill you, you creep!

[*Struggle continues,* BENNIE *pinning her arms under his legs as he kneels over her on the bed.* ARLENE *is terrified and in pain.*]

BENNIE: You will? You'll kill ol Bennie . . . kill ol Bennie like you done that cabdriver?

[*A cruel reminder he employs to stun and mock her.* ARLENE *looks as though she has been hit.* BENNIE *is still fired up, he unzips his pants.*]

ARLENE: [*Passive, cold and bitter*] This how you got your Dorrie, rapin?

BENNIE: [*Unbuttoning his shirt*] That what you think this is, rape?

ARLENE: I oughta know.

BENNIE: Uh-huh.

ARLENE: First they unzip their pants.

[BENNIE *pulls his shirt out.*]

ARLENE: Sometimes they take off their shirt. But mostly, they just pull it out and stick it in.

[BENNIE *stops, one hand goes to his fly, finally hearing what she has been saying. He straightens up, obviously shocked. He puts his arms back in his shirt.*]

BENNIE: Don't you call me no rapist. [*Pause, then insistent*] No, I ain't no rapist, Arlie. [*Gets up, begins to tuck his shirt back in and zip up his pants.*]

ARLENE: And I ain't Arlie.

[ARLENE *remains on the bed as he continues dressing.*]

BENNIE: No, I guess you ain't.

ARLENE: [*Quietly and painfully*] Arlie coulda killed you.

END OF ACT I

These announcements will be heard during the last five minutes of the intermission.

LOUDSPEAKER: Garden workers will, repeat, will, report for work this afternoon. Bring a hat and raincoat and wear boots. All raincoats will be checked at the front gate at the end of work period and returned to you after supper.

Your attention please. A checkerboard was not returned to the recreation area after dinner last night. Anyone with information regarding the black and red checkerboard missing from the recreation area will please contact Mrs. Duvall after lunch. No checkerboards or checkers will be distributed until this board is returned.

Betty Rickey and Mary Alice Wolf report to the laundry. Doris Creech and Arlie Holsclaw report immediately to the superintendent's office. The movie this evening will be *Dirty Harry* starring Clint Eastwood. Doris Creech and Arlie Holsclaw report to the superintendent's office immediately.

The bus from St. Mark's this Sunday will arrive at one P.M. as usual. Those residents expecting visitors on that bus will gather on the front steps promptly at one-twenty and proceed with the duty officer to the visiting area after it has been confirmed that you have a visitor on the bus.

Attention all residents. Attention all residents. [*Pause*] Mrs. Helen Carson has taught needlework classes here at Pine Ridge for thirty years. She will be retiring at the end of this month and moving to Florida where her husband has bought a trailer park. The resident council and the superintendent's staff has decided on a suitable retirement present. We want every resident to participate in this project—which is—a quilt, made from scraps of material collected from the residents and sewn together by residents and staff alike. The procedure will be as follows: A quilting room has been set up in an empty storage area just off the infirmary. Scraps of fabric will be collected as officers do evening count. Those residents who would enjoy cutting up old uniforms and bedding no longer in use should sign up for this detail with your dorm officer. If you would like to sign your name or send Mrs. Carson some special message on your square of fabric, the officers will have tubes of embroidery paint for that purpose. The backing for the quilt has been donated by the Women's Associates as well as the refreshments for the retirement party to be held after lunch on the thirtieth. Thank you very much for your attention and participation in this worthwhile tribute to someone we are all very fond of here. You may resume work at this time. Doris Creech and Arlie Holsclaw report to the superintendent's office immediately.

Act II

[*The next morning.* ARLENE *is asleep on the bed.* ARLIE *is locked in a maximum security cell. We do not see the officer to whom she speaks.*]

ARLIE: No, I don't have to shut up, neither. You already got me in seg-re-ga-tion, what else you gonna do? I got all day to sleep, while everbody else is out bustin ass in the laundry. [*Laughs*] Hey! I know . . . you ain't gotta go do no dorm count, I'll just tell you an you jus sit. Huh? You preciate that? Ease them corns you been moanin about. . . . Yeah . . . O.K. Write this down. [*Pride, mixed with alternating contempt and amusement*] Startin down by the john on the back side, we got Mary Alice. Sleeps with her pillow stuffed in her mouth. Says her mom says it'd keep her from grindin down her teeth or somethin. She be suckin that pillow like she gettin paid for it. [*Laughs*] Next, it's Betty the Frog. Got her legs all opened out like some fuckin. . . . [*Makes croaking noises.*] Then it's Doris eatin pork rinds. Thinks somebody gonna grab em outta her mouth if she eats em during the day. Doris ain't dumb. She fat, but she ain't dumb. Hey! You notice how many girls is fat here? Then it be Rhonda, snorin, Marvene, wheezin and Suzanne, coughin. Then Clara an Ellie be still whisperin. Family shit, who's gettin outta line, which girls is gittin a new work 'signment, an who kin git extra desserts an for how much. Them's the two really run this place.

51

My bed right next to Ellie, for sure it's got some of her shit hid in it by now. Crackers or some crap gonna leak out all over my sheets. Last time I found a fuckin grilled cheese in my pillow. Even had two of them little warty pickles. Christ! O.K. Linda and Lucille. They be real quiet, but they ain't sleepin. Prayin, that's them. Linda be sayin them "Hell Mary's" till you kin just about scream. An Lucille, she tol me once she didn't believe in no God, jus some stupid spirits whooshin aroun everwhere makin people do stuff. Weird. Now, I'm goin back down the other side, there's. . . . [*Screams*] I'd like to see you try it! I been listenin at you for the last three hours. Your husband's gettin laid off an your lettuce is gettin eat by rabbits. Crap City. *You* shut up! Whadda I care if I wake everybody up? I want the nurse. . . . I'm gettin sick in here . . . an there's bugs in here!

[*The light comes up in the apartment. Faint morning traffic sounds are heard.* ARLENE *does not wake up. The* WARDEN *walks across the catwalk. The* GUARD *catches up with him near* ARLIE'*s cell.* BENNIE *is stationed at the far end of the walk.*]

LOUDSPEAKER: Dorm A may now eat lunch.

GUARD: Warden, I thought four-five-six . . . [*Nodding in* ARLIE'*s direction*] was leavin here.

WARDEN: Is there some problem?

GUARD: Oh, we can take care of her all right. We're just tired of takin her shit, if you'll pardon the expression.

ARLIE: [*Interrupting*] You ain't seen nuthin yet, you mother.

WARDEN: Washington will decide on her transfer. Til then, you do your job.

GUARD: She don't belong here. Rest of—

LOUDSPEAKER: [*Interrupts him.*] Betty Rickey and Mary Alice Wolf report to the laundry.

GUARD: Most of these girls are mostly nice people, go along with things. She needs a cage.

ARLIE: I need a knife. [*Vicious*]

WARDEN: Had it occurred to you that we could send the

rest of them home and just keep her? [*Very curt. Walks away.*]

LOUDSPEAKER: Dorm A may now eat lunch. A Dorm to lunch.

GUARD: [*Turning around, muttering to himself*] Oh, that's a swell idea. Let everbody out except bitches like Holsclaw.
[*She makes an obscene gesture at him. He turns back toward the catwalk.*]

GUARD: Smartass Warden, thinks he's runnin a hotel.

BENNIE: [*Having overheard this last interchange*] Give you some trouble, did she?

GUARD: I can wait.

BENNIE: For what?

GUARD: For the day she tries gettin out an I'm here by myself. I'll show that screechin slut a thing or two.

BENNIE: That ain't the way, Evans.

GUARD: The hell it ain't. Beat the livin—

BENNIE: Outta a little thing like her? Gotta do her like all the rest. You git your shorts washed by givin Betty Rickey Milky Ways. You git your chairs fixed givin Frankie Hill extra time in the shower with Lucille Smith. An you git ol Arlie girl to behave herself with a stick of gum. Gotta have her brand, though.

GUARD: You screwin that wildcat?

BENNIE: [*Starts walk to* ARLIE's *cell.*] Watch.
[ARLIE *is silent as he approaches, but is watching intently.*]

BENNIE: Now, [*To nobody in particular*] where was that piece of Juicy Fruit I had in this pocket. Gotta be here somewhere. [*Takes a piece of gum out of his pocket and drops it within* ARLIE's *reach.*] Well, [*Feigning disappointment*] I guess I already chewed it.
[ARLIE *reaches for the gum and gets it.*]

BENNIE: Oh, [*Looking down at her now*] how's it goin, kid?

ARLIE: O.K.
[ARLIE *says nothing, but unwraps the gum and chews*

it. BENNIE *leaves the cell area, motioning to the* OTHER
GUARD *as if to say, "See, that's how it's done."*
A loud siren goes by in the street below the apartment.
ARLENE *bolts up out of bed, then turns back to it
quickly, making it up in a frenzied, ritual manner. As
she tucks the spread up under the pillow, the siren
stops and so does she. For the first time, now, she looks
around the room, realizing where she is and the habit
she has just played out.*
*A jackhammer noise gets louder. She walks over to the
window and looks out. There is a wolf whistle from a
worker below. She shuts the window in a fury, then
grabs the bars. She starts to shake them, but then her
hand goes limp. She looks around the room, as if trying
to remember what she is doing there. She looks at her
watch, now aware that it is late and that she has slept
in her clothes.*]

ARLENE: People don't sleep in their clothes, Arlene. An
    people git up fore noon.
    [ARLENE *makes a still-disoriented attempt to pull her-
    self together, changing shoes, combing her hair, wash-
    ing her face, etc., as* GUARDS *and other prison life con-
    tinues on the catwalk.*]

WARDEN: [*Walking up to* ARLIE, *remaining some distance
    from her, but talking directly to her, as he appears to
    check files or papers*] Good afternoon, Arlie.

ARLIE: Fuck you. [WARDEN *walks away.*]

ARLIE: Wait! I wanna talk to you.

WARDEN: I'm listening.

ARLIE: When am I gittin outta here?

WARDEN: That's up to you.

ARLIE: The hell it is.

WARDEN: When you can show that you can be with the
    other girls, you can get out.

ARLIE: How'm I supposed to prove that bein in here?

WARDEN: And then you can have mail again and visitors.

ARLIE: You're just fuckin with me. You ain't ever gonna

let me out. I been in this ad-just-ment room four months, I think.

WARDEN: Arlie, you see the other girls on the dorm walking around, free to do whatever they want? If we felt the way you seem to think we do, everyone would be in lockup. When you get out of segregation, you can go to the records office and have your time explained to you.

ARLIE: It won't make no sense.

WARDEN: They'll go through it all very slowly ... when you're eligible for parole, how many days of good time you have, how many industrial days you've earned, what constitutes meritorious good time ... and how many days you're set back for your write-ups and all your time in segregation.

ARLIE: I don't even remember what I done to git this lockup.

WARDEN: Well, I do. And if you ever do it again, or anything like it again, you'll be right back in lockup where you will stay until you forget *how* to do it.

ARLIE: What was it?

WARDEN: You just remember what I said.

ARLENE: Now, then ... [*Sounds as if she has something in mind to do. Looks as though she doesn't.*]

ARLIE: What was it?

WARDEN: Oh, and Arlie, the prison chaplain will be coming by to visit you today.

ARLIE: I don't want to see no chaplain.

WARDEN: Did I ask you if you wanted to see the chaplain? No, I did not. I said, the chaplain will be coming by to visit you today. Mrs. Roberts, why hasn't this light bulb been replaced? [*To an unseen* GUARD. *Walks away.*]

ARLIE: [*Screaming*] Get out of my hall!

[WARDEN *walks away.*

ARLENE *walks to the refrigerator and opens it. She picks out a carton of slaw* BENNIE *put there last night. She walks away from the door, then turns around, re-*

membering to close it. She looks at the slaw, as GUARD
comes up to ARLIE'*s cell with a plate.*]

ARLENE: I ain't never eatin no more scrambled eggs.

GUARD: Chow time, cutie pie.

ARLIE: These eggs ain't scrambled, they's throwed up!
And I want a fork!

[ARLENE *realizes she has no fork, then fishes one out
of the garbage sack from last night. She returns to the
bed, takes a bite of slaw and gets her wallet out of her
purse. She lays the bills out on the bed one at a time.*]

ARLENE: That's for coffee . . . and that's for milk and bread
. . . an that's cookies . . . an cheese an crackers . . . an
shampoo an soap . . . an bacon an liver cheese. No,
pickle loaf . . . an ketchup and some onions . . . an peanut butter an jelly . . . an shoe polish. Well, ain't no
need gettin everything all at once. Coffee, milk, ketchup, cookies, cheese, onions, jelly. Coffee, milk . . .
oh, shampoo . . .

RUBY [*Off*]: [*Banging on the door, yelling*] Candy, I gotta
have my five dollars back.

ARLENE: [*Quickly stuffing her money back in her wallet*]
Candy ain't here!

RUBY: It's Ruby upstairs. She's got five dollars I loaned
her . . . Arlie? That Arlie? Candy told me her sister be . . .
[ARLENE *opens the door hesitantly*]

RUBY: It is Arlie, right?

ARLENE: It's Arlene. [*Does not extend her hand.*]

RUBY: See, I got these shoes in layaway . . . [*Puts her
hand back in her pockets.*] She said you been . . . you
just got . . . you seen my money?

ARLENE: No.

RUBY: I don't get em out today they go back on the shelf.

ARLENE: [*Doesn't understand.*] They sell your shoes?

RUBY: Yeah. Welcome back.

ARLENE: Thank you. [*Embarrassed, but relieved*]

RUBY: She coulda put it in my mailbox.

[RUBY *starts to leave,* ARLENE *is closing the door behind her, when* RUBY *turns around.*]

RUBY: Uh ... listen ... if you need a phone, I got one most of the time.

ARLENE: I do have to make this call.

RUBY: Ain't got a book though. . . . Well, I got one but it's holdin up my bed. [*Laughs*]

ARLENE: I got the number.

RUBY: Well, then ... [*Awkward*]

ARLENE: Would you ... wanna come in?

RUBY: You sure I'm not interruptin anything?

ARLENE: I'm sposed to call my parole officer.

RUBY: Good girl. Most of them can't talk but you call em anyway.

[ARLENE *does not laugh.*]

RUBY: Candy go back to that creep?

ARLENE: I guess.

RUBY: I's afraid of that. [*Looking around*] Maybe an envelope with my name on it? Really cleaned out the place, didn't she?

ARLENE: Yeah. Took everything.

[*They laugh a little.*]

RUBY: Didn't have much. Didn't do nuthin here 'cept ... sleep.

ARLENE: Least the rent's paid til the end of the month. I'll be workin by then.

RUBY: You ain't seen Candy in a while.

ARLENE: No. Think she was in the seventh grade when ...

RUBY: She's growed up now, you know.

ARLENE: Yeah. I was thinkin she might come by.

RUBY: Honey, she won't be comin by. He keeps all his ... [*Starting over*] His place is pretty far from here. But ... [*Stops, trying to decide what to say.*]

ARLENE: But what?

RUBY: But she had a lot of friends, you know. *They* might be comin by.

ARLENE: Men, you mean.

RUBY: Yeah. [*Quietly, waiting for* ARLENE's *reaction*]

ARLENE: [*Realizing the truth*] Mother said he was her boyfriend.

RUBY: I shouldn't have said nuthin. I jus didn't want you to be surprised if some john showed up, his tongue hangin out an all. [*Sits down on the bed.*]

ARLENE: It's O.K. I shoulda known anyway. [*Now suddenly angry.*] No, it ain't O.K. Guys got their dirty fingernails all over her. Some pimp's out buying green pants while she. . . . Goddamn her.

RUBY: Hey now, that ain't your problem. [*Moves toward her,* ARLENE *backs away.*]

ARLIE: [*Pointing*] You stick your hand in here again Doris an I'll bite it off.

RUBY: She'll figure it out soon enough.

ARLIE: [*Pointing to another person*] An you, you ain't my mama, so you can cut the mama crap.

ARLENE: I wasn't gonna cuss no more.

RUBY: Nuthin in the parole rules says you can't git pissed. My first day outta Gilbertsville I done the damn craziest . . .

[ARLENE *looks around, surprised to hear* RUBY *has done time.*]

RUBY: Oh yeah, a long time ago, but . . . hell, I heaved a whole gallon of milk right out the window my first day.

ARLENE: [*Somewhat cheered*] It hit anybody?

RUBY: It bounced! Made me feel a helluva lot better. I said, "Ruby, if a gallon of milk can bounce back, so kin you."

ARLENE: That's really what you thought?

RUBY: Well, not exactly. I had to keep sayin it for bout a year fore I finally believed it. I's moppin this lady's floor once an she come in an heard me sayin "gallon-a'-milk, gallon-a'-milk." Fired me. She did. Thought I was too crazy to mop her floors.

[*Laughs, but is still bitter.* ARLENE *wasn't listening.* RUBY *wants to change the subject now.*]

RUBY: Hey! You have a good trip? Candy said you was in Arkansas.

ARLENE: Alabama. It was O.K. This guard, well he used to be a guard, he just quit. He ain't never seen Kentucky, so he drove me. [*Watching for* RUBY's *response*]

RUBY: Pine Ridge?

ARLENE: Yeah.

RUBY: It's coed now, ain't it?

ARLENE: Yeah. That's dumb, you know. They put you with men so's they can git you if you're seen with em.

RUBY: Sposed to be more natural, I guess.

ARLENE: I guess.

RUBY: Well, I say it sucks. Still a prison. No matter how many pictures they stick up on the walls or how many dirty movies they show, you still gotta be counted five times a day. [*Now beginning to worry about* ARLENE's *silence*] You don't seem like Candy said.

ARLENE: She tell you I was a killer?

RUBY: More like the meanest bitch that ever walked. I seen lots worse than you.

ARLENE: I been lots worse.

RUBY: Got to you, didn't it?

[ARLENE *doesn't respond, but* RUBY *knows she's right.*]

RUBY: Well, you jus gotta git over it. Bein out, you gotta—

ARLENE: Don't you start in on me.

RUBY: [*Realizing her tone*] Right, sorry.

ARLENE: It's O.K.

RUBY: Ex-cons is the worst. I'm sorry.

ARLENE: It's O.K.

RUBY: Done that about a year ago. New waitress we had. Gave my little goin straight speech, "No booze, no men, no buyin on credit," shit like that, she quit that very night. Stole my fuckin raincoat on her way out. Some speech, huh? [*Laughs, no longer resenting this theft.*]

ARLENE: You a waitress?

RUBY: I am the Queen of Grease. Make the finest French fries you ever did see.

ARLENE: You make a lot of money?

RUBY: I sure know how to. But I ain't about to go back inside for doin it. Cookin out's better'n eatin in, I say.

ARLENE: You think up all these things you say?

RUBY: Know what I hate? Makin salads—cuttin up all that stuff 'n floppin it in a bowl. Some day ... some day ... I'm gonna hear "tossed salad" an I'm gonna do jus that. Toss out a tomato, toss out a head a' lettuce, toss out a big ol carrot. [*Miming the throwing act and enjoying herself immensely*]

ARLENE: [*Laughing*] Be funny seein all that stuff flyin outta the kitchen.

RUBY: Hey Arlene! [*Gives her a friendly pat.*] You had your lunch yet?

ARLENE: [*Pulling away immediately*] I ain't hungry.

RUBY: [*Carefully*] I got raisin toast.

ARLENE: No. [*Goes over to the sink, twists knobs as if to stop a leak.*]

ARLIE: Whaddaya mean, what did she do to me? You got eyes or is they broke? You only seein what you feel like seein. I git ready to protect myself from a bunch of weirdos an then you look.

ARLENE: Sink's stopped up. [*Begins to work on it.*]

ARLIE: You ain't seein when they's leavin packs of cigarettes on my bed an then thinking I owe em or somethin.

RUBY: Stopped up, huh? [*Squashing a bug on the floor.*]

ARLIE: You ain't lookin when them kitchen workers lets up their mommies in line nights they know they only baked half enough brownies.

RUBY: Let me try.

ARLIE: You ain't seen all the letters comin in an goin out with visitors. I'll tell you somethin. They's one of them workmen buries dope for Betty Rickey in little plastic bottles under them sticker bushes at the water tower. You see that? No, you only seein me. Well, you don't see shit.

RUBY: [*A quiet attempt*] Gotta git you some Drano if you're gonna stay here.

ARLIE: I'll tell you what she done. Doris brung me some rollers from the beauty school class. Three fuckin pink rollers. Them plastic ones with the little holes. I didn't ask her. She jus done it.

RUBY: Let me give her a try.

ARLENE: I can fix my own sink.

ARLIE: I's stupid. I's thinkin maybe she were different from all them others. Then that night everbody disappears from the john and she's wantin to brush my hair. Sure, brush my hair. How'd I know she was gonna crack her head open on the sink? I jus barely even touched her.

RUBY: [*Walking to the bed now, digging through her purse*] Want a Chiclet?

ARLIE: You ain't asked what she was gonna do to me. Huh? When you gonna ask that? You don't give a shit about that cause Doris such a good girl.

ARLENE: Don't work. [*Giving up*]

RUBY: We got a dishwasher quittin this week if you're interested.

ARLENE: I need somethin that pays good.

RUBY: You type?

ARLENE: No.

RUBY: Do any clerk work?

ARLENE: No.

RUBY: Any keypunch?

ARLENE: No.

RUBY: Well, then I hate to tell you, but all us old-timers already got all the good cookin and cleanin jobs.
[*Smashes another bug, goes to the cabinet to look for the bug spray.*]
She even took the can of Raid! Just as well, empty anyway.
[ARLENE *doesn't respond.*]

RUBY: She hit the bugs with it.
[*Still no response.*]

RUBY: Now, there's that phone call you was talkin about.

ARLENE: Yeah.

RUBY: [*Walking toward the door*] An I'll git you that

number for the dishwashin job, just in case.

[ARLENE *backs off.*]

RUBY: How bout cards? You play any cards? Course you do. I get sick of beatin myself all the time at solitaire. Damn borin bein so good at it.

ARLENE: [*Goes for her purse.*] Maybe I'll jus walk to the corner an make my call from there.

RUBY: It's always broke.

ARLENE: What?

RUBY: The phone . . . at the corner. Only it ain't at the corner. It's inside the A & P.

ARLENE: Maybe it'll be fixed.

RUBY: Look, I ain't gonna force you to play cards with me. It's time for my programs anyway.

ARLENE: I gotta git some pickle loaf an . . . things.

RUBY: Suit yourself. I'll be there if you change your mind.

ARLENE: I have something to do here first.

RUBY: [*Trying to leave on a friendly basis*] Look, I'll charge you a dime if it'll make you feel better.

ARLENE: [*Takes her seriously.*] O.K.

RUBY: [*Laughs, then realizes* ARLENE *is serious.*] Mine's the one with the little picture of Johnny Cash on the door. [*Walks to the door and leaves.*]

[BENNIE's *singing begins almost immediately, as* AR-LENE *walks toward the closet. She is delaying going to the store, but is determined to go. She checks little things in the room, remembers to get a scarf, changes shoes, checks her wallet, finally, as she is walking out, she stops and looks at the picture of Jesus, then moves closer, having noticed a dirty spot. She goes back into the bathroom for a tissue, wets it in her mouth, then dabs at the offending spot. She puts the tissue in her purse then leaves the room when noted.*]

BENNIE: [*To the tune of "I'll Toe the Line," while carrying a tray of paper cups and a pitcher of water across the catwalk.*] I keep my pants up with a piece of twine. I keep my eyes wide open all the time, Da da da

da-da da da da da da [*Doesn't know this line.*] If you'll
be mine, please pull the twine.

ARLIE: You can't sing for shit.

BENNIE: You know what elephants got between their
toes?

ARLIE: I don't care.

BENNIE: Slow natives. [*Laughs*]

ARLIE: That ain't funny.

GUARD: Hey, Davis. [*As* BENNIE *opens the cell and walks
in*]

BENNIE: Conversation is rehabilitatin, Evans. Want some
water?

ARLIE: O.K.

BENNIE: How bout some Kool-Aid to go in it? [*Gives her
a glass of water.*]

ARLIE: When does the chaplain come?

BENNIE: Want some gum?

ARLIE: Is it today?

BENNIE: Kool-Aid's gone up, you know. Fifteen cents and
tax. You get out, you'll learn all about that.

ARLIE: Does the chaplain come today?

BENNIE: Income tax, sales tax, property tax, gas and elec-
tric, water, rent . . .

ARLIE: Hey!

BENNIE: Yeah, he's comin, so don't mess up.

ARLIE: I ain't.

BENNIE: What's he tell you anyway, get you so starry-
eyed?

ARLIE: He jus talks to me.

BENNIE: I talk to you.

ARLIE: Where's Frankie Hill?

BENNIE: Gone.

ARLIE: Out?

BENNIE: Pretty soon.

ARLIE: When.

BENNIE: Miss her don't you? Ain't got nobody to bullshit
with. Stories you gals tell. . . . Whoo-ee!

ARLIE: Get to cut that grass now, Frankie, honey.

BENNIE: Huh?

ARLIE: Stupidest thing she said. [*Gently*] Said first thing she was gonna do when she got out . . .

[ARLENE *leaves the apartment.*]

BENNIE: Get laid.

ARLIE: Shut up. First thing was gonna be going to the garage. Said it always smelled like car grease an turpur . . . somethin.

BENNIE: Turpentine.

ARLIE: Yeah, an gasoline, wet. An she'll bend down an squirt oil in the lawn mower, red can with a long pointy spout. Then cut the grass in the back yard, up an back, up an back. They got this grass catcher on it. Says she likes scoopin up that cut grass an spreadin it out under the trees. Says it makes her real hungry for some lunch. [*A quiet curiosity about all this.*]

BENNIE: I got a power mower, myself.

ARLIE: They done somethin to her. Took out her nerves or somethin. She—

BENNIE: She jus got better, that's all.

ARLIE: Hah. Know what else? They give her a fork to eat with last week. A fork. A fuckin fork. Now how long's it been since I had a fork to eat with?

BENNIE: Wish I could help you with that, honey.

ARLIE: Don't call me honey. [*Loud.*]

BENNIE: That's my girl.

ARLIE: I ain't your girl.

BENNIE: Screechin wildcat.

ARLIE: What time is it? [*Very quiet.*]

[ARLENE *walks back into the apartment. She is out of breath and has some trouble getting the door open. She is carrying a big sack of groceries. As she sets the bag on the counter, it breaks open, spilling cans and packages all over the floor. She just stands and looks at the mess. She takes off her scarf and sets down her purse, still looking at the spilled groceries. Finally, she bends down and picks up the package of pickle loaf.*]

She starts to put it on the counter, then turns suddenly and throws it at the door. She stares at it as it falls.]

ARLENE: Bounce? [*In disgust*)] Shit.

[ARLENE *sinks to the floor. She tears open the package of pickle loaf and eats a piece of it, tearing off the bites in her mouth. She is still angry, but is completely unable to do anything about her anger.*]

ARLIE: Who's out there? Is anybody out there? [*Reading*] Depart from evil and do good. [*Yelling*] Now, you pay attention out there cause this is right out of the Lord's mouth. [*Reading*] And dwell, that means live, dwell for-ever-more. [*Speaking*] That's like for longer than I've been in here or longer than.... This Bible the chaplain give me's got my name right in the front of it. Hey! Somebody's sposed to be out there watchin me. Wanna hear some more? [*Reading*] For the Lord for— [*The word is forsaketh.*] I can't read in here, you turn on my light, you hear me? Or let me out and I'll go read it in the TV room. Please let me out. I won't scream or nuthin. I'll just go right to sleep, O.K.? Somebody! I'll go right to sleep. O.K.? You won't even know I'm there. Hey! Goddammit, somebody let me out of here, I can't stand it in here any more. Somebody!

ARLENE: [*Finally, she draws her knees up, wraps her arms around them and rests her head on her arms.*] Jus gotta git a job an make some money an everything will be all right. You hear me, Arlene? You git yourself up an go find a job. [*Continues to sit.*] An you kin start by cleanin up this mess you made cause food don't belong on the floor. [*Still sitting.*]

[CARL *appears in the doorway of the apartment. When he sees* ARLENE *on the floor, he goes into a fit of vicious, sadistic laughter.*]

CARL: What's happenin, Mama? You havin lunch with the bugs?

ARLENE: [*Quietly*] Fuck off.

CARL: [*Threatening*] What'd you say?

ARLENE: [*Reconsidering*] Go away.

CARL: You watch your mouth or I'll close it up for you. [ARLENE *stands up now.* CARL *goes to the window and looks out, as if checking for someone.*]

ARLENE: They after you, ain't they?
[CARL *sniffs, scratches at his arm. Finding a plastic bag near the bed, stuffed with brightly colored knitted things. He pulls out baby sweaters, booties and caps.*]

CARL: What the fuck is this?

ARLENE: You leave them be.

CARL: You got a baby hid here somewhere? I foun its little shoes. [*Laughs, dangling them in front of him.*]

ARLENE: Them's mine. [*Chasing him*]

CARL: Aw sugar, I ain't botherin nuthin. Just lookin. [*Pulls more out of the sack, dropping one or two on the floor, kicking them away with his feet.*]

ARLENE: [*Picking up what he's dropped*] I ain't tellin you again. Give me them.

CARL: [*Turns around quickly, walking away with a few of the sweaters.*] How much these go for?

ARLENE: I don't know yet.

CARL: I'll jus take care of em for you—a few coin for the trip. You *are* gonna have to pay your share, you know.

ARLENE: You give me them. I ain't goin with you. [*She walks toward him.*]

CARL: You ain't?
[*Mocking,* ARLENE *walks up close to him now, taking the bag in her hands. He knocks her away and onto the bed.*]

CARL: Straighten up, girlie. [*Now kneels over her.*] You done forgot how to behave yourself. [*Moves as if to threaten her, but kisses her on the forehead, then moves out into the room.*]

ARLENE: [*Sitting up*] I worked hard on them things. They's nice, too, for babies and little kids.

CARL: I bet you fooled them officers good, sittin around doin this shit. [*Throws the bag in the sink.*]

ARLENE: I weren't . . .

CARL: [*Interrupting*] I kin see that scene. They sayin . . .

[*Puts on a high southern voice.*] "I'd jus love one a' them nice yella sweaters."

ARLENE: They liked them.

CARL: Those turkeys, sure they did. Where else you gonna git your free sweaters an free washin an free step-right-up-git-your-convict-special-shoe-shine. No, don't give me no money, officer. I's jus doin this cause I likes you. [*Uncle Tom talk*]

ARLENE: They give em for Christmas presents.

CARL: [*Checks the window again, then peers into the grocery sack.*] What you got sweet, Mama? [*Pulls out a box of cookies and begins to eat them.*]

ARLIE: I'm sweepin, Doris, cause it's like a pigpen in here. So you might like it, but I don't, so if you get some mops, I'll take one of them, too.

ARLENE: You caught another habit, didn't you?

CARL: You turned into a narc or what?

ARLENE: You scratchin an sniffin like crazy.

CARL: I see a man eatin cookies an that's what you see too.

ARLENE: An you was laughin at me sittin on the floor! You got cops lookin for you an you ain't scored yet this morning. You better git yourself back to prison where you can git all you need.

CARL: Since when Carl couldn't find it if he really wanted it?

ARLENE: An I bought them cookies for me.

CARL: An I wouldn't come no closer if I's you.

ARLENE: [*Stops, then walks to the door.*] Then take the cookies and git out.

CARL: [*Imitating* BENNIE] Oh, please, Miss Arlene, come go with Carl to the big city. We'll jus have us the best time.

ARLENE: I'm gonna stay here an git a job an save up money so's I kin git Joey. [*Opening the door*] Now, I ain't sposed to see no ex-cons.

CARL: [*Big laugh*] You don't know nobody else. Huh, Arlie? Who you know ain't a "con-vict"?

ARLENE: I'll meet em.

CARL: And what if they don't wanna meet you? You ain't exactly a nice girl, you know. An you gotta be jivin about that job shit. [*Throws the sack of cookies on the floor.*]

ARLENE: I kin work. [*Retrieving the cookies*]

CARL: Doin what?

ARLENE: I don't know. Cookin, cleanin, somethin that pays good.

CARL: You got your choice, honey. You can do cookin an cleanin or you can do somethin that pays good. You ain't gonna git rich working on your knees. You come with me an you'll have money. You stay here, you won't have shit.

ARLENE: Ruby works an she does O.K.

CARL: You got any Kool-Aid? [*Looking in the cabinets, moving* ARLENE *out of his way*] Ruby who?

ARLENE: Upstairs. She cooks. Works nights an has all day to do jus what she wants.

CARL: And what, exactly, do she do? See flicks? Take rides in cabs to pick up see-through shoes?

ARLENE: She watches TV, plays cards, you know.

CARL: Yeah, I know. Sounds just like the dayroom in the fuckin joint.

ARLENE: She likes it.

CARL: [*Exasperated*] All right. Say you stay here an *finally* find yourself some job. [*Grabs the picture of Jesus off the wall.*] This your boyfriend?

ARLENE: The chaplain give it to me.

CARL: Say it's dishwashin, O.K.?

[ARLENE *doesn't answer.*]

CARL: O.K.?

ARLENE: O.K. [*Takes the picture, hangs it back up.*]

CARL: An you git maybe seventy-five a week. Seventy-five for standin over a sinkful of greasy gray water, fishin out blobs of bread an lettuce. People puttin pieces of chewed-up meat in their napkins and you gotta pick it out. Eight hours a day, six days a week, to make seventy-five lousy pictures of Big Daddy George. Now, how long it'll take you to make seventy-five workin for me?

ARLENE: A night. [*Sits on the bed,* CARL *pacing in front of her.*]

CARL: Less than a night. Two hours maybe. Now, it's the same fuckin seventy-five bills. You can either work all week for it or make it in two hours. You work two hours a night for me an how much you got in a week?

[ARLENE *looks puzzled by the multiplication required.* CARL *sits down beside her, even more disgusted.*]

CARL: Two seventy-fives is one-fifty. Three one-fifties is four-fifty. You stay here you git seventy-five a week. You come with me an you git four-fifty a week. Now, four-fifty, Arlie, is *more* than seventy-five. You stay here you gotta work eight hours a day and your hands git wrinkled and your feet swell up. [*Suddenly distracted*] There was this guy at Bricktown had webby toes like a duck. [*Back now*] You come home with me you work two hours a night an you kin sleep all mornin an spend the day buyin eyelashes an tryin out perfume. Come home, have some guy openin the door for you sayin, "Good evenin, Miss Holsclaw, nice night now ain't it?" [*Puts his arm around her.*]

ARLENE: It's Joey I'm thinkin about.

CARL: If you was a kid, would you want your mom to git so dragged out washin dishes she don't have no time for you an no money to spend on you? You come with me, you kin send him big orange bears an Sting-Ray bikes with his name wrote on the fenders. He'll like that. Holsclaw. [*Amused*] Kinda sounds like coleslaw, don't it? Joey be tellin all his friends bout his mom livin up in New York City an bein so rich an sendin him stuff all the time.

ARLENE: I want to be with him.

CARL: [*Now stretches out on the bed, his head in her lap.*] So, fly him up to see you. Take him on that boat they got goes roun the island. Take him up to the Empire State Building, let him play King Kong. [*Rubs her hair, unstudied tenderness.*] He be talkin bout that trip his whole life.

ARLENE: [*Smoothing his hair*] I don't want to go back to prison, Carl.

CARL: [*Jumps up, moves toward the refrigerator.*] There any chocolate milk? [*Distracted again*] You know they got this motel down in Mexico named after me? Carl's Bad Cabins. [*Proudly*] Who said anything about goin back to prison? [*Slams the refrigerator door.*] What do you think I'm gonna be doin? Keepin you out, that's what!

ARLENE: [*Stands up.*] Like last time? Like you gettin drunk? Like you looking for kid junkies to beat up?

CARL: God, ain't it hot in this dump. You gonna come or not? You wanna wash dishes, I could give a shit. [*Now yelling*] But you comin with me, you say it right now, lady! [*Grabs her by the arm.*] Huh?

RUBY: [*Knocks on the door.*] Arlene?

CARL: She ain't here! [*Yelling*]

RUBY: Arlene! You all right?

ARLENE: That's Ruby I was tellin you about.

CARL: [*Catches her arm again, very rough.*] We ain't through!

RUBY: [*Opening the door*] Hey! [*Seeing the rough treatment*] Goin to the store. [*Very firm*] Thought maybe you forgot somethin.

CARL: [*Turns ARLENE loose.*] You this cook I been hearin about?

RUBY: I cook. So what?

CARL: Buys you nice shoes, don't it, cookin? Why don't you hock your watch an have somethin done to your hair? If you got a watch.

RUBY: Why don't you drop by the coffee shop. I'll spit in your eggs.

CARL: They let you bring home the half-eat chili dogs?

RUBY: You . . . you got half-eat chili dogs for brains. [*To

ARLENE] I'll stop by later. [*Contemptuous look for* CARL]

ARLENE: No. Stay.

[CARL *gets the message.*]

CARL: [*Goes over to the sink to get a drink of water out of the faucet, then looks down at his watch.*] Piece a' shit. [*Thumps it with his finger.*] Shoulda took the dude's hat, jack. Guy preachin about the end of the world ain't gonna own a watch that works.

ARLENE: [*Walks over to the sink, bends over* CARL.] You don't need me. I'm gittin too old for it, anyway.

CARL: I don't discuss my business with strangers in the room. [*Heads for the door.*]

ARLENE: When you leavin?

CARL: Six. You wanna come, meet me at this bar. [*Gives her a brightly colored matchbook.*] I'm havin my wheels delivered. [*With faintly uncertain pride*]

ARLENE: You stealin a car?

CARL: Take a cab. [*Gives her a dollar.*] You don't come . . . well, I already laid it out for you. I ain't never lied to you, have I girl?

ARLENE: No.

CARL: Then you be there. That's all the words I got. [*Makes an unconscious move toward her.*] I don't beg nobody. [*Backs off.*] Be there.

[*Turns abruptly and leaves.* ARLENE *watches him go, folding up the money in the matchbook. The door remains open.*]

ARLIE: [*Reading from a small testament*] Depart from evil and do good. And dwell forevermore. For the Lord forsaketh not his Saints, but the seed of the wicked shall be cut off.

RUBY: [*Walks over to the counter, starts to pick up some of the groceries lying on the floor, then stops.*] I 'magine you'll want to be putting these up yourself.

[ARLENE *continues to stare out the door.*]

RUBY: He do this?

ARLENE: No.

RUBY: Can't trust these sacks. I seen bag boys punchin holes in em at the store.

ARLENE: Can't trust anybody. [*Finally turning around*]

RUBY: Well, you don't want to trust him, that's for sure.

ARLENE: We spent a lot of time together, me an Carl.

RUBY: He live here?

ARLENE: No, he jus broke outta Bricktown near where I was. I got word there sayin he'd meet me. I didn't believe it then, but he don't lie, Carl don't.

RUBY: You thinkin of goin with him?

ARLENE: They'll catch him. I told him but he don't listen.

RUBY: Funny ain't it, the number a' men come without ears.

ARLENE: How much that dishwashin job pay?

RUBY: I don't know. Maybe seventy-five.

ARLENE: That's what he said.

RUBY: He tell you you was gonna wear out your hands and knees grubbin for nuthin, git old an be broke an never have a nice dress to wear? [*Sitting down*]

ARLENE: Yeah.

RUBY: He tell you nobody's gonna wanna be with you cause you done time?

ARLENE: Yeah.

RUBY: He tell you your kid gonna be ashamed of you an nobody's gonna believe you if you tell em you changed?

ARLENE: Yeah.

RUBY: Then he was right. [*Pauses.*] But when you make your two nickels, you can keep both of em.

ARLENE: [*Shattered by these words*] Well, I can't do that.

RUBY: Can't do what?

ARLENE: Live like that. Be like bein dead.

RUBY: You kin always call in sick . . . stay home, send out for pizza an watch your Johnny Carson on TV . . . or git a bus way out Preston Street an go bowlin . . .

ARLENE: [*Anger building*] What am I gonna do? I can't git no work that will pay good cause I can't do nuthin. It'll be years fore I have a nice rug for this place. I'll

never even have some ol Ford to drive around, I'll
never take Joey to no fair. I won't be invited home for
pot roast and I'll have to wear this fuckin dress for the
rest of my life. What kind of life is that?

RUBY: It's outside.

ARLENE: Outside? Honey I'll either be inside this apartment or inside some kitchen sweatin over the sink.
Outside's where you get to do what you want, not
where you gotta do some shit job jus so's you can eat
worse than you did in prison. That ain't why I quit bein
so hateful, so I could come back and rot in some slum.

RUBY: [*Word "slum" hits hard*] Well, you can wash
dishes to pay the rent on your "slum," or you can
spread your legs for any shit that's got the ten dollars.
[*With obvious contempt*]

ARLENE: [*Now hostile*] An I don't need you agitatin me.

RUBY: An I don't live in no slum.

ARLENE: [*Sensing* RUBY's *hurt*] Well, I'm sorry ... it's
just ... I thought ... [*Increasingly upset*]

RUBY: [*Finishing her sentence for her*] ... it was gonna
be different. Well, it ain't. And the sooner you believe
it, the better off you'll be.

ARLIE: Where's the chaplain? I got somethin to tell him.

ARLENE: They said I's ...

GUARD: He ain't comin.

ARLENE: ... he tol me if ... I thought once Arlie ...

ARLIE: It's Tuesday. He comes to see me on Tuesday.

GUARD: Chaplain's been transferred, dollie. Gone. Bye-
bye. You know.

ARLENE: He said the meek, meek, them that's quiet and
good ... the meek ... as soon as Arlie ...

RUBY: What, Arlene? Who said what?

ARLIE: He's not comin back?

ARLENE: At Pine Ridge there was ...

ARLIE: He woulda told me if he couldn't come back.

ARLENE: I was ...

GUARD: He left this for you.

ARLENE: I was ...

GUARD: Picture of Jesus, looks like.

ARLENE: . . . this chaplain . . .

RUBY: Arlene . . . [*Trying to call her back from this hysteria*]

ARLIE: [*Hysterical*] I need to talk to him. [*Guard leaves*]

ARLENE: This chaplain . . .

ARLIE: You tell him to come back and see me. [*Pleading*]

ARLENE: I was in lockup . . .

ARLIE: I want the chaplain! [*Screaming*]

ARLENE: I don't know . . . years . . .

RUBY: And . . .

ARLENE: This chaplain said I had . . . said Arlie was my hateful self and she was hurtin me and God would find some way to take her away. . . . And it was God's will so I could be the meek . . . the meek, them that's quiet and good an git whatever they want . . . I forgit that word . . . they git the Earth.

RUBY: Inherit.

ARLENE: Yeah. And that's why I done it.

RUBY: Done what?

ARLENE: What I done. Cause the chaplain he said . . . I'd sit up nights waitin for him to come talk to me.

RUBY: Arlene, what did you do? What are you talkin about?

ARLENE: They tol me . . . after I's out an it was all over . . . they said after the chaplain got transferred . . . I didn't know why he didn't come no more til after. . . . They said it was three whole nights at first, me screamin to God to come git Arlie an kill her. They give me this medicine an thought I's better. . . . Then that night it happened, the officer was in the dorm doin count . . . an they didn't hear nuthin but they come back out where I was an I'm standin there tellin em to come see, real quiet I'm tellin em, but there's all this blood all over my shirt an I got this fork I'm holdin real tight in my hand . . . [*Clenches one hand now, the other hand fumbling with the buttons as if she's going to show* RUBY.] this fork, they said Doris stole it from the kitchen an

give it to me so I'd kill myself and shut up botherin her
... an there's all these holes all over me where I been
stabbin myself an I'm sayin Arlie is dead for what she
done to me, Arlie is dead an it's God's will ... I didn't
scream it, I was jus sayin it over an over ... Arlie is
dead, Arlie is dead ... they couldn't git that fork outta
my hand til ... I woke up in the infirmary an they said
I almost died. They said they's glad I didn't. [*Smiling*]
They said did I feel better now an they was real nice,
bringing me chocolate puddin ...

RUBY: I'm sorry, Arlene. [*Reaches out for her, but AR-*
LENE pulls away sharply.]

ARLENE: I'd be eatin or jus lookin at the ceiling an git a
tear in my eye, but it'd jus dry up, you know, it didn't
run out or nuthin. An then pretty soon, I's well, an
officers was sayin they's seein such a change in me an
givin me yarn to knit sweaters an how'd I like to have
a new skirt to wear an sometimes lettin me chew gum.
They said things ain't never been as clean as when I's
doin the housekeepin at the dorm. [*So proud*] An then
I got in the honor cottage an nobody was foolin with
me no more or nuthin. And I didn't git mad like before
or nuthin. I just done my work an knit.... An I don't
think about it what happened, cept ... [*Now losing*
control] People here keep callin me Arlie an ... [*Has*
trouble saying "Arlie"] I didn't mean to do it, what I
done ...

RUBY: Oh, honey ... [*Trying to help*]

ARLENE: I did ... [*This is very difficult.*] I mean, Arlie
was a pretty mean kid, but I did ... [*Very quickly*] I
didn't know what I ... Arlie! [*Breaks down com-*
pletely, screaming, crying, falling over into RUBY's *lap.*]

RUBY: [*Rubs her back, her hair, waiting for the calm she*
knows will come. Finally, but very quietly.] You can
still ... [*Now obviously referring to some personal loss*
of her own] ... you can still love people that's gone.
[RUBY *continues to hold her tenderly, rocking as with*
a baby.

A terrible crash is heard on the steps outside the apartment.]

BENNIE'S VOICE: Well, chicken-pluckin, shit!

RUBY: Don't you move now, it's just somebody out in the hall.

ARLENE: That's . . .

RUBY: It's O.K., Arlene. Everything's gonna be just fine. Nice and quiet now.

ARLENE: That's Bennie that guard I told you about.

RUBY: I'll get it. You stay still now. [*She walks to the door, and looks out into the hall, hands on hips.*] Why you dumpin them flowers on the stairs like that? Won't git no sun at all! [*Turns back to* ARLENE.] Arlene, there's a man plantin a garden out in the hall. You think we should call the police or get him a waterin' can?

BENNIE: [*Appearing in the doorway, carrying a box of dead-looking plants*] I didn't try to fall, you know.

RUBY: Well, when you git ready to try, I wanna watch! [*Blocking the door*]

ARLENE: I thought you's gone.

RUBY: [*To* BENNIE] You got a visitin pass?

BENNIE: [*Coming into the room*] Arlie . . . [*Quickly*] Arlene. I brung you some plants. You know, plants for your window. Like we talked about, so's you don't see them bars.

RUBY: [*Picking up one of the plants*] They sure is scraggly lookin things. Next time, git plastic.

BENNIE: I'm sorry I dropped em, Arlene. We kin get em back together an they'll do real good. [*Setting them down on the trunk*] These ones don't take the sun. I asked just to make sure. Arlene?

RUBY: You up for seein this petunia killer?

ARLENE: It's O.K. Bennie, this is Ruby, upstairs.

BENNIE: [*Bringing one flower over to show* ARLENE, *stuffing it back into its pot*] See? It ain't dead.

RUBY: Poor little plant. It comes from a broken home.

BENNIE: [*Walks over to the window, getting the box and*

holding it up to the window.] That's gonna look real
pretty. Cheerful-like.

RUBY: Arlene ain't gettin the picture yet. [*Walking to the
window and holding her plant up, too, posing*] Now.
[ARLENE *looks, but is not amused.*]

BENNIE: [*Putting the plants back down*] I jus thought,
after what I done last night . . . I jus wanted to do
somethin nice.

ARLENE: [*Calmer now*] They is nice. Thanks.

RUBY: Arlene says you're a guard.

BENNIE: I was. I quit. Retired.

ARLENE: Bennie's goin back to Alabama.

BENNIE: Well, I ain't leavin right away. There's this guy
at the motel say the bass is hittin pretty good right now.
Thought I might fish some first.

ARLENE: Then he's goin back.

BENNIE: [*To* RUBY *as he washes his hands*] I'm real fond
of this little girl. I ain't goin til I'm sure she's gonna do
O.K. Thought I might help some.

RUBY: Arlene's had about all the help she can stand.

BENNIE: I got a car, Arlene. An money. An . . . [*Reaching
into his pocket*] I brung you some gum.

ARLENE: That's real nice, too. And I preciate what you
done, bringin me here an all, but . . .

BENNIE: Well, look. Least you can take my number at the
motel an give me a ring if you need somethin. [*Gives
her a piece of paper.*] Here, I wrote it down for you.
[ARLENE *takes the paper.*]

BENNIE: Oh, an somethin else, these towel things . . .
[*Reaching into his pocket, pulling out the packaged
towelettes*] they was in the chicken last night. I thought
I might be needin em, but they give us new towels
ever day at that motel.

ARLENE: O.K. then. I got your number.

BENNIE: [*Backing up toward the door*] Right. Right. Any
ol thing, now. Jus any ol thing. You even run outta gum
an you call.

RUBY: Careful goin down.

ARLENE: Bye Bennie.

BENNIE: Right. The number now. Don't lose it. You know, in case you need somethin.

ARLENE: No.

[BENNIE *leaves,* ARLENE *gets up and picks up the matchbook* CARL *gave her and holds it with* BENNIE's *piece of paper.*]

RUBY: [*Watches a moment, sees* ARLENE *trying to make this decision, knowing that what she says now is very important.*] We had this waitress put her phone number in matchbooks, give em to guys left her nice tips. Anyway, one night this little ol guy calls her and comes over and says he works at this museum an he don't have any money but he's got this hat belonged to Queen Victoria. An she felt real sorry for him so she screwed him for this little ol lacy hat. Then she takes the hat back the next day to the museum thinkin she'll git a reward or somethin an you know what they done? [*Pause*] Give her a free membership. Tellin her thanks so much an we're so grateful an wouldn't she like to see this mummy they got downstairs . . . an all the time jus stallin . . . waiting cause they called the police.

ARLENE: You do any time for that?

RUBY: [*Nods yes*] County jail.

ARLENE: [*Tears up the matchbook and drops it into the garbage can, mouthing the words "County jail".*] You got any Old Maids?

RUBY: Huh?

ARLENE: You know.

RUBY: Cards? [*Surprised and pleased*]

ARLENE: [*Laughs a little.*] It's the only one I know.

RUBY: Old Maid, huh? [*Not her favorite game*]

ARLENE: I gotta put my food up first.

RUBY: Bout an hour?

ARLENE: I'll come up.

RUBY: Great. [*Stopping by the plants on her way to the door*] These plants is real ugly.

[*Fondly. Exits.*

ARLENE *watches her, then turns back to the groceries still on the floor. Slowly, but with great determination, she picks up the items one at a time and puts them away in the cabinet above the counter.*

ARLIE *appears on the catwalk, one light on each of them.*]

ARLIE: Hey! You remember that time we was playin policeman an June locked me up in Mama's closet an then took off swimmin? An I stood around with them dresses itchin my ears an crashin into that door tryin to git outta there? It was dark in there. So, finally, [*Very proud*] I went around an peed in all Mama's shoes. But then she come home an tried to git in the closet only June taken the key so she said, "Who's in there?" an I said, "It's me!" an she said, "What you doin in there?" and I started gigglin an she started pullin on the door an yellin, "Arlie, what you doin in there?" [*Big laugh*]

ARLIE *and* ARLENE: [ARLENE *has begun to smile during the story, now they say together, both standing as Mama did, one hand on her hip.*] Arlie, what you doin in there?

ARLENE: [*Still smiling and remembering, stage dark except for one light on her face.*] Aw shoot. [*Light dims on her fond smile as* ARLIE *laughs once more.*]

THE END

BARD BOOKS

DISTINGUISHED DRAMA

THE ALCESTIAD Thornton Wilder	41855	2.25
ARMS AND THE MAN George Bernard Shaw	01628	.60
CANDIDE Lillian Hellman	12211	1.65
THE CHANGING ROOM, HOME, **THE CONTRACTOR: THREE PLAYS** David Storey	22772	2.45
DANTON'S DEATH Georg Büchner	10876	1.25
A DREAM PLAY August Strindberg	18655	.75
EQUUS Peter Shaffer	24828	1.75
THE FANTASTICKS Tom Jones and Harvey Schmidt	22129	1.65
GHOSTS Henrik Ibsen	22152	.95
HEDDA GABLER Henrik Ibsen	24620	.95
THE INSPECTOR GENERAL Nikolai Gogol	28878	.95
THE IMPORTANCE OF BEING EARNEST Oscar Wilde	46771	1.50
THE LOWER DEPTHS Maxim Gorky	18630	.75
MISS JULIE August Strindberg	36855	.95
OUR TOWN Thornton Wilder	45732	1.75
THE PLAYBOY OF THE WESTERN WORLD John Millington Synge	22046	.95
THE CHERRY ORCHARD Anton Chekhov	36848	.95
THE SEA GULL Anton Chekhov	24638	.95
THE SHADOW BOX Michael Cristofer	46839	2.25
THREE PLAYS BY THORNTON WILDER Thornton Wilder	48231	2.25
UNCLE VANYA Anton Chekhov	18663	.75
THE WILD DUCK Henrik Ibsen	23093	.95
WOYZECK Georg Büchner	10751	1.25

Where better paperbacks are sold, or directly from the publisher. Include 50¢ per copy for mailing; allow 4-6 weeks for delivery.

Avon Books, Mail Order Dept.
224 W. 57th St., New York, N.Y. 10019

BDD 10-79